Changing English

NATIONAL CURRICULUM KEY STAGE 3

CHRIS DAVIES   HAZEL HAGGER

Longman

contents

SKILLS SESSIONS

 This means there is a Copymaster in the *Teacher's File*.

National Curriculum English

This book will help you to learn a great deal of the skills and knowledge that you will need to have in order to do well in English as part of the National Curriculum.

On the left hand sides of these pages, you can see the full range of abilities and knowledge that you will be learning between the ages of eleven and fourteen. It will help you a great deal if you know the kinds of things you're meant to be learning in English.

On the right hand sides of these pages, you can see which particular sections of this book will help you with the different things you need to do in English:

We hope you *enjoy* working on this book – and that it really does help you to do well in English.

SPEAKING AND LISTENING

- talk about an event, a personal experience or an activity in a way that other people can follow

Focusing on experience

- contribute to discussions, listen to what other people say, and be willing to discuss other people's points of view, be willing to put forward your own point of view, and to argue a case for it

Influencing people

- use language to pass on and explain information and ideas to other people so that they understand what you mean

Managing information

- help plan a group discussion, and take part in it, take part in a group presentation or performance

Different kinds of English
Focusing on experience
Influencing people

- notice the different ways of using the English language that are going on around you all the time – the different words that people use, and their different ways of speaking – because of what they do, or where they come from

Different kinds of English

- know and use some of the terms which describe how language works – such as *noun, verb, sentence, paragraph, dialect, accent, Standard* and *non-standard English*

Different kinds of English
Skills Sessions

READING

- read aloud from books in a lively and expressive way

Telling stories

- read stories, and talk about how they have been written, how they work, and what you think of them

Telling stories
Pleasures and preferences

- speak or write about the things you like to read, watch or listen to, and explain what it is you like about them

Pleasures and preferences

- when discussing things that you read, watch or listen to, show that you can tell the difference between fact and opinion

Influencing people

- know some of the history of the English language

  Different kinds of English

- find out information that you need from reference books and other information materials, use contents lists and indexes to find the answers to your own questions

  Managing information

- find the books or other materials that you need in a library

  Managing information

- read a wide range of books – *novels, diaries, autobiographies and other non-fiction, books from other countries*

  Pleasures and preferences
  Focusing on experience

WRITING

- do different kinds of writing – *stories, poems, letters, notes, instructions, reviews, newspaper articles, autobiography* – for a wide range of readers, use these many kinds of writing in order to *entertain, explain, inform, think about ideas, persuade and express your own feelings and beliefs*

  Different kinds of English
  Telling stories
  Managing information
  Pleasures and preferences
  Focusing on experience
  Influencing people

- use punctuation such as full stops, capital letters, commas and speech punctuation, brackets and dashes so that your writing is easy to understand

  Skills Sessions
  Copymasters

- use a variety of connecting words in your writing in order to give it a clear and helpful structure

  Copymaster

- be able to write in Standard English, know about and make use of some of the different ways language can be used in speaking and in writing, and about some of the reasons for using English in different ways

  Different kinds of English
  Influencing people

- write impersonally when necessary, using language that hides how you really feel

  Influencing people
  Skills Session

- put your ideas together – on paper, on a computer screen, or in discussion with others – and show that you know how to produce a first draft from your ideas

  Telling stories
  Focusing on experience

- revise and redraft your writing, on your own and with the help of other people

  Telling stories
  Focusing on experience
  Influencing people

- talk about and use different kinds of language for different purposes, different subjects, and different readers or listeners

  Different kinds of English
  Influencing people

PRESENTATION

- spell increasingly difficult words correctly in the things you write, and understand some of ways in which English spelling works

  Skills Sessions
  Copymasters

- check your final drafts of writing for incorrect spellings

  Copymasters

- present finished work clearly and attractively, and in different ways for different purposes

  Managing information
  Pleasures and preferences
  Influencing people

different kinds of English

Contents

Introduction

In this Project, you are going to find out about some of the different kinds of English that people use. You will see what's different about them, and why they are different. You will learn how to recognise and talk about many of them, including Standard English.

You are going to investigate the different kinds of English that go on in your school, and you'll find out about why the English language can be used in different ways.

Products

You will collect together lots of language examples – examples of the different ways that the English language is used by pupils, teachers, and everyone else in your school. You'll put all the things you've found out into a School Language Guide.

Audience

Your School Language Guide will help people who don't know the English language as well as you do to make sense of all the different ways people speak and write in your school.

In other words, it will be for foreigners – this Guide will be something you can give to any foreign visitors who come to your school, to help them understand what's going on.

The work you do for this Project will be extremely useful.

1 The languages of school

Soundbites

If you walked round your school for a while, you would hear language being used in very many different ways. Schools are bursting with language – the *English* language – being used in all sorts of different ways for all sorts of different reasons.

> **1** Imagine you are invisible. Think of some of the things you could hear if you walked around school for an hour or two, just listening.

Imagine, for instance, what the following people in the following situations might be saying:

- one pupil shouting to another along a corridor;
- a cookery teacher to a first year class;
- the headteacher to a pupil who keeps turning up late;
- an English teacher handing out a book of poems to a class;
- two pupils playing hockey (on the same team);
- the caretaker to one of the cleaners during a coffee break;
- a maths teacher to a pupil she's throwing out of a lesson;
- one pupil to another behind the bike sheds;
- fifth year pupils in a motor mechanics class, surrounded by dismantled engine parts;
- the deputy head giving a talk in assembly;
- a dance and drama teacher with a second year class;
- a third year pupil asking a strict teacher for permission to leave the room.

2   Write down your ideas of what these people would be saying. You can't write down *everything* they'd say, of course, so just put together a collection of **soundbites**. Soundbites should be *short* – anything from one to twenty-five words at most and they should catch the feel of how someone speaks.
Title this: 'School Soundbites' and lay it out like the example below.

One kid shouting to another in corridor: 'Wotcha Sprogsy!'

Cookery teacher to first years: 'Now I want you ALL to listen VERY carefully to what I have to say about *hygiene*.'

3   Compile a class collection of real school soundbites over the next couple of days. Compare these with the ones you made up. How accurate were those guesses you made?

If everyone in the class manages to jot down three things that they hear around school – the typical sorts of things that one hears in school – in the form of soundbites, then you can put together a big display of school language. It could be illustrated with drawings, and possibly photos taken from a school brochure or magazine.

Slang

Slang uses invented words, which outsiders often can't understand. Slang words are fun. They are not part of the serious kind of language that you are usually taught in school. Slang is language that people make up for themselves.

Some slang words become a regular part of the language – but they still confuse people who don't live in England. For example:

> A *quid* = £1, *bloke* = man.

Some more modern slang words are also becoming part of the language, but plenty of people in this country probably don't know them:

> *wimp* = weedy person
> *hacker* = someone who knows how to break into computer systems
> *ligger* = someone who hangs around expensive places for free food and drink

Everyone occasionally uses slang, but nobody uses it quite so often, or so well, as schoolchildren. You are the experts on slang words.

For example: fifteen years ago, schoolchildren in at least one secondary school in Oxfordshire liked to use the word *wheelie* for when teachers lost their tempers.

> 'He's having a real *wheelie*.' (everyone laughs, teacher gives up)

This was at a time when motorbikes were particularly popular and the sport of motorcycling had built up a lot of specialist terms.

The pupils in that school took the word wheelie from motorcycling and applied it to teachers, to describe how, when they got cross, they would sort of rev up and go up in the air (quite an accurate description, in some cases). This term wheelie was popular in that school for about a year, and then it disappeared. Some slang words just last for a few months, and some words become part of the language.

1   In pairs or small groups, talk about any slang words that you know of. These can be words that are used a lot by all sorts of different people and sometimes even on television. Make a list of them, showing:

■ what they mean;
■ where you heard them being used.

2   Make a list of any slang words that are used a lot in your school. They might be words that were actually made up by people in your school. Explain what they mean.

3   Write a short conversation between a few friends talking together during the dinner-hour at school, in which they use a lot of slang. This can be a private conversation, that other people are not meant to understand.

Write this like a story, describing where they are and what they're doing. You'll need to use **speech punctuation** for this.

If you are unsure of how to do this,
go to Skills Session 1, How to punctuate speech on page 157.

Correct English

Does your English teacher ever correct your English? That's what English teachers are meant to do, after all. They teach you correct English.

When you write things in school, teachers often try to help you get rid of the mistakes that you make: they try to show you the correct way to write English. In other words, they are showing you how to use **Standard English**.

1 Look through your English exercise books or folders, and see if you can find any corrections that your English teacher has made to your writing when marking your work.
    See how many different kinds of correction you can find: e.g. spelling, punctuation, layout, grammar, slang, etc.
    Try to figure this out for yourself first, and then ask your English teacher to explain anything you're not sure about.
    Write a list of the kinds of mistake that you often make in your writing, and keep this for your School Language Guide.

2 Discuss with your English teacher what he or she thinks about the following questions:

   ■ Do you think it is important to correct mistakes we make in our writing? Why?
   ■ Do you always correct every mistake? If not, why not?
   ■ What kinds of mistakes in our writing bother you most? Why?
   ■ How do you try to teach pupils not to make these mistakes?
   ■ Do you think it is important to correct the way we speak (all the time, sometimes, never)?
   ■ Why do you think that?

You will probably want to do this as a whole class discussion. Perhaps one member of the class could chair the discussion, and allow other members of the class to ask the different questions. It would be useful if you all took notes about what your English teacher says, because this will also be something important to put in your School Language Guide.

When English teachers correct your writing, or the way you speak, it is most likely that they are teaching you how to use Standard English. In fact, a good way of explaining what Standard English actually is, is to say:

STANDARD ENGLISH IS WHAT YOU ARE TAUGHT IN SCHOOL.

2 Seeing English from the outside

At least 400 million people, across the world, learn English as a foreign language. These are people born in countries all around the world who grow up speaking their own language (e.g. French, Arabic, Chinese, Italian, Spanish, Greek and so on), and who want to know English at some time in their lives.

People come to this country at one time or another for various reasons:

- for a holiday;
- to study;
- to work for a short while;
- to settle down and live here.

Often, when foreigners come to Britain, they discover that there are far more ways of using the English language than they were able to learn about in their own countries. English is a rich and complicated language, and it comes in many different versions. Foreigners come across three main difficulties when they come to this country.

Accent and pronunciation

The way that people **pronounce** words – the sounds they use – are called **accents**. There are lots of different accents in this country (such as Cockney, Welsh, Yorkshire, etc). Foreigners can't learn about all of them before they come here.

Also, no matter what accent people speak with, they often speak in ways that are difficult for foreigners to understand. They speak too quickly, and they don't always pronounce all the sounds in words clearly. This can make life difficult for a foreigner.

Vocabulary

However hard they work at their English studies, foreign learners cannot hope to learn as many English words as most native English speakers know by the time they are ten or eleven years old. Foreigners come across words that are new to them, such as technical words, slang words, newly invented words all the time. For example:

lap-top = a lightweight, portable computer
trendy   = someone who keeps up with the latest fashions
twitcher = a very keen bird-watcher
yuppy   = a smart young person who earns a lot of money
zapper   = someone who uses a remote control to keep changing TV channels

Background knowledge

People who have lived somewhere for a long time know what's going on, and don't need to explain things to each other all the time. They share a lot of **background knowledge** which is a complete mystery to an outsider about things like what they watch on TV or what's been happening in the news or the names of shops, of food, of transport.

Foreign visitors don't know about these things, and often find it hard to follow what's going on.

Most of all they don't share your background knowledge about the different ways people in this country speak. You'll find the same things happening to you when you go abroad.

1   Discuss the difficulties a foreigner might have in coping with the way people speak in this country. Use the following questions to help you:

   ■ What things might foreigners who have just arrived in Britain find hard to understand during a day in a big city?
   ■ What things on television or radio might foreigners find hard to understand?
   ■ What kinds of talking in your school might foreigners find hard to understand?

2 Improvise a short drama scene. Decide which parts each of you will play, talk about the things that will happen, and work it out as you go along.

The situation you are going to act out will involve foreign visitors to your school, such as pupils on an exchange, or a new teacher from abroad. These visitors can't understand some of the school language that they hear being used, and things begin to get embarrassing. This will involve about five to six of you in each group:

- one or two foreigner visitors, who have learnt *some* English in their own countries;
- two to three British people (pupils, teachers, cafeteria staff) speaking to, or in front of, the foreigners in a way which they can't understand;
- one British person who tries to help.

REMEMBER: **accent**, **vocabulary**, **background knowledge**.

3 Now that you have some idea of the problems that foreigners come across when they first hear the English language being used in a real-life setting like school, you can start to prepare your School Language Guide.

The first thing to do is to make a folder in which you can put all the bits and pieces about language you are going to collect throughout this Project. It would be a good idea to make a very attractive cover, which clearly explains what's going to be inside the folder.

You should already have some good school language examples to put into it, which you kept from the work you did in the last section.

3 Standard English

Using words clearly

Look at the following extract from a story called 'A Table is a Table' by Peter Bichsel, about a man who gets so fed up with life that he decides it is time for a change – so he changes the way he uses language:

'Always the same table,' said the man, 'the same chairs, the bed, the picture. And the table I call table, the picture I call picture, the bed is called bed, and the chair is called chair. Why, come to think of it? The French call a bed "lee", a table "tahbl", call a picture "tahblow" and a chair "shaze", and they understand each other. And the Chinese understand each other too.'

'Why isn't the bed called picture?' thought the man, and smiled, then he laughed, laughed till the neighbours banged on the wall and shouted 'Quiet!'

'Now things are going to change,' he cried out, and from now on he called the bed 'picture'.

'I'm tired, I want to go to picture,' he said, and often in the morning he would lie in picture for a long time, wondering what he would now call the chair, and he called the chair 'alarm clock'.

So he got up, dressed, sat down on his alarm clock and rested his arms on the table. But the table was no longer called table, it was now called carpet. So in the morning the man left his picture, got dressed, sat down at the carpet on the alarm clock and wondered what to call that.

He called the bed picture.

He called the table carpet.

He called the chair alarm clock.

He called the mirror chair.

He called the alarm clock photograph album.

He called the wardrobe newspaper.

He called the carpet wardrobe.

He called the picture table.

And he called the photograph album mirror.

So: In the morning the old man would lie in picture for a long time, at nine the photograph album rang, the man got up and stood on the wardrobe, so that his feet wouldn't feel cold, then he took his clothes out of the newspaper, dressed, looked into the chair on the wall, then sat down on the alarm clock at the carpet and turned the pages of the mirror until he found his mother's table.

The man thought this was fun, and he practised all day long and impressed the words on his memory. Now he gave everything new names: Now he was no longer a man, but a foot, and the foot was a morning and the morning a man.

It is possible to make sense of what this old man did with words, if some words stay the same, or if you have the key to his special language. But it should hardly come as a surprise to you that, at the end of the story, none of the old man's friends can understand a word he says – and so nobody speaks to him any more.

Try this for yourself – do some writing in which you change words around from the way we *normally* use them. Choose one of the three following topics to write about – but don't tell anyone else which one you've chosen, so that they've got to try and work it out for themselves:

■ cooking a meal,
■ going shopping for some new clothes,
■ going on a journey.

You might find it helps you to write the story first using words normally. Then you can invent your own code and rewrite the piece using words with your own special meanings.

If everybody made up their own private meaning for words, nobody would ever understand each other. Language can only work if people agree on how to use it. Over the course of hundreds of years, a **standardised** version of our language has been worked out, so that everyone can know what words mean. That's what *dictionaries* are for – to tell us what the agreed meanings of words actually are.

Standardised means to agree on a way of doing something so that everyone does it in the same way – like making electrical plugs all the same size, or using railway lines of the same width.

One of the reasons for standardising the way we use language, therefore, is:

IT AIDS CLEAR COMMUNICATION, AND PREVENTS CONFUSION, IF WE ALL USE LANGUAGE IN THE SAME WAY.

See Skills Session 2, Language commands (page 158) and Skills Session 4, Nouns and adjectives (page 160).

Spelling properly

Even very badly misspelt words can usually be understood if you say them out loud. Then you *hear* what the person meant, even if it isn't immediately obvious to the eye. Read this piece of writing by a twelve year old school pupil, for example:

> ### The Balte of Wacster
>
> I wos on my hase the Balelt begun someone Bule of a derteygrat gun, my mate wos hit in the are and the hed and he fell to graund, and of cuse he wos ded a nuther was het with a fliping grat stick a nuther was hit and a nuther wos Hit

When you *look* at that writing, it seems quite impossible to understand – but when you try to say it out loud, it does become clear quite quickly (it helps if you know that it is a poem).

Purfick speling iz not issenshal – yu ken yugeli figger owt wot sumwun meenz evun wen vey avunt a cloo ow ter spel – but it can waste a lot of time.

People often find bad spelling annoying. This is sometimes simply because they have to slow down and read more carefully. But sometimes it's for another kind of reason. Incorrect spelling annoys some people simply *because* it is incorrect. They might be able to understand a misspelt word perfectly well, but they *disapprove* of the fact that it is wrong.

SOME PEOPLE HAVE A BAD OPINION OF YOU IF YOU DON'T USE THE LANGUAGE ACCURATELY.

Ask some adult that you know – preferably someone who has firm standards about how people should behave – whether they think it is important to spell words correctly, and why. Ask them if it ever *annoys* them when people spell things wrong.
Discuss your findings in your next English lesson. What sort of spelling mistakes annoy them? Why?

Using formal language

The rules of language are not just about practical, straightforward things like spelling. There are also rules about what is, and is not, *acceptable* in language – and that includes the way you *speak* as well as the way you *write*.

SPEAKING CHILDISHLY

Very young children, who are just beginning to learn to talk, can get away with saying anything they want to – like announcing on a bus that they've 'just done a poo, dad', or saying 'that man's got a big nose, haha'. But you can't get away with that kind of thing for long. It's the job of parents to teach their children how to make sense, and not to go around offending people with the way they talk. Part of growing up, and learning how to get on in the world, involves learning about how to say the right thing, at the right time.

Children learn very quickly that there are occasions in life when you have to use language carefully – when you have to *dress up* your language a bit, just like putting on your best clothes, to make a good impression.

> Make up a short story about a young child being taught how to behave properly, which can involve looking neat, doing the right things, and saying the right things.

Write about something that might actually have happened to you once. Think of some occasion when grown-ups taught you to behave properly, and to talk properly:

- a visit to grandparents, or neighbours;
- a wedding, or some other ceremony;
- going to the doctor or dentist.

This story is about the way people talk, so **dialogue** will be very important. Use **speech punctuation**.

SPEAKING IN A GROWN-UP WAY

There are certain extremely **formal** occasions in life when people expect you to use language in a formal way. For instance:

- swearing an oath in a court of law;
- getting married;
- promising to do something: it isn't enough, sometimes, just to say 'OK then' – you actually have to say 'I promise' sometimes;
- talking on the phone to a stranger: you have to announce who you are, and what you want, and you have to be more than usually careful about saying goodbye;
- apologising sincerely.

These are formal situations, because there are certain things that you are *always* meant to do. One of the things you are meant to do in formal situations is to *say the right kinds of words*.

The things you are meant to say have become standardised – apologising sincerely is a particularly good example of this. How do you make clear to someone that you are really sorry for something you have done? Often there is no way of avoiding actually saying you're sorry in a very formal way – by saying the right and proper words for the occasion. It is often only by using the correct way of apologising that you can bring an unpleasant incident to a close.

Write two versions of a letter of apology to a neighbour that you have offended, or annoyed, a great deal. You decide what it was that you might have done wrong.
First write a formal version, using all the proper language of apology.
Secondly try to write another version, this time without using any of the normal language of apology.

You might well find that it simply is not possible to make a proper apology unless you use the formal apologising words that have become standardised in our language.

What is Standard English?

There are many different ways of describing **Standard English**.

- You can talk about certain *rules* of language. For example:
    'I haven't done it' is Standard English.
    'I ain't done it' breaks the rules of Standard English – it is non-standard English.
- You can talk about *when* Standard English is meant to be used. For example: in writing, in education, in the media, in formal situations like job interviews and weddings and law courts, etc.
- You can talk about people's *attitudes* to Standard English – what they think of it. For example: people think it shows that you're educated, that you're polite, etc.
- You can talk about where it came from – the *history* of Standard English. For example: the rules of Standard English were first written down in the eighteenth century.

The important thing is to understand that there is a particularly important version of English called Standard English and that there are times when everyone needs to be able to use it.

Write some advice for a foreign visitor to England who wants to find examples of Standard English being used. Imagine that the foreign visitor wants to spend just one day looking for examples of Standard English being used in this country.

- What places should they go to?
- What people should they listen to?
- What should they read?
- What should they listen to on the radio, or watch on television?

You could plan out a whole day's timetable that would provide your visitor with the most chances possible of coming across Standard English being used. This will be included in the School Language Guide.

A brief history of English

The information that follows will tell you the story of Standard English. This story begins in the fifth century. We are now at the end of the twentieth century, and the English language has spent all that time growing, and taking shape. That makes 1500 years of non-stop change.

FIFTH CENTURY

In the fifth century, invaders from the countries that we now know as the Netherlands, Germany and Denmark came to this country. These people were known as Angles, Saxons and Jutes. They took over large parts of Britain, and their languages started to be used there. Before that, people had spoken Celtic languages, which now survive only in Scotland, Wales and Cornwall.

A new language grew up in this country during the next few hundred years. We now call this either Anglo-Saxon or *Old English*. Old English has many differences from the language we use, but once you were used to it, you'd still be able to recognise words that we use today.

EIGHTH CENTURY

Old English had been spoken for long enough by this time for people to start using it to write books. Old English varied quite a lot from one part of the country to another, and the version that was used for writing was from the West Saxon part of England. You can see where that is on this map.

During this century there were a lot of Viking raids, from Denmark. Many new words came into the language as a result. Many missionaries came to the country as well, spreading Christianity. They introduced a lot of Latin words into the language.

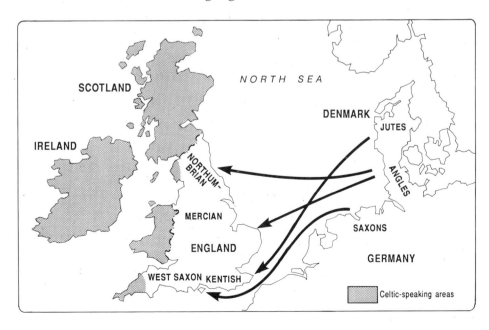

ELEVENTH CENTURY

In 1066, William the Conqueror led an invasion from Normandy in France. This was the last major invasion of Britain. The French language was used by the people who ran the country, and after a while that began to change the English language very much.

FOURTEENTH CENTURY

The French language had mixed in with Old English. Old English disappeared and what we now call *Middle English* took over. This was much more like the English language that we use now.

The most famous writer who used Middle English was Geoffrey Chaucer, who wrote *The Canterbury Tales*. He lived in London, and spoke the English that was used in that part of the country – East Midlands English. You can see where that was spoken on this map.

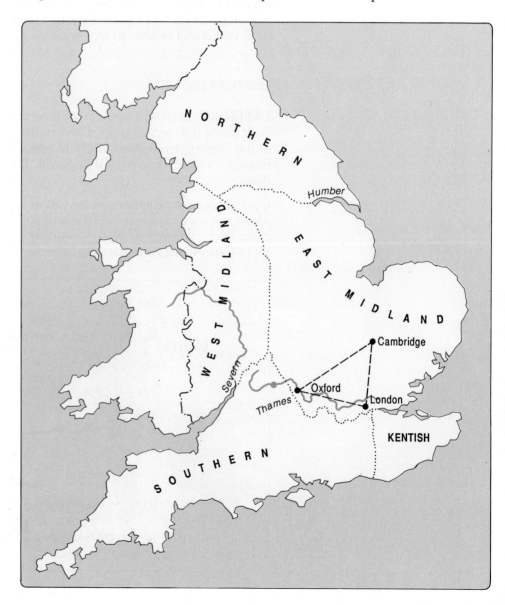

FIFTEENTH CENTURY

William Caxton started printing in this country. He worked in London, and like Chaucer, he used the East Midlands version of English.

This was also the version of Middle English that was spoken by the people who ran the government in London, and by the people at the universities of Oxford and Cambridge. It isn't surprising that the East Midlands version of English became the kind of English we use now – became Standard English.

SIXTEENTH CENTURY

People from this country were voyaging all around the world by now and they brought back new words from all the different languages they heard on their travels.

During this century, William Shakespeare wrote his plays. Although he used some words that aren't the same now, it isn't too difficult to understand what he wrote nowadays, four hundred years after he wrote his plays. Shakespeare's plays are written in an early version of *modern English*.

SEVENTEENTH CENTURY

Like the Angles, Saxons, Jutes and Normans had done hundreds of years earlier, British people set off round the world and began to take control of many countries. Because of that, English is spoken in countries all round the world: America, Australia, New Zealand, the Indian sub-continent, East and West Africa, Malaysia, parts of China, and many more places.

EIGHTEENTH CENTURY

In this century, Standard English was finally worked out and agreed on. People wrote dictionaries and grammars that laid down rules about what words should mean, and how we should write and spell the English language. The kind of English that was standardised during this century is still more or less the same, two hundred years later, although we don't use all the rules that were invented then any more.

TWENTIETH CENTURY

English is now a very important language all around the world. This is largely because it is used in America. American English is very like British English, but there are many small differences.

In Britain, there has been large-scale immigration into this country for the last fifty years from the Indian sub-continent, East and West Africa, Hong Kong and the Caribbean. People from other European countries have also come to live here.

English isn't the only language used in this country – an exciting and varied range of other languages are also spoken by a great number of people: Punjabi, Bengali, Urdu, Gujarati, German, Polish, Italian, Greek and Spanish.

Language is continuing to change in all sorts of ways. More and more people are learning to read and write, which gives them a much better opportunity to get on in life. Micro-technology and word processors are changing the way we use language almost as much as the printing press did in the fifteenth century. Television and high speed travel are spreading the English language, and all other languages, around the world. Every language will change as a result of this. Language – the English language, and all languages – has certainly not finished changing.

Try to find short examples of the way English was used in as many of the centuries mentioned in this brief history as possible.
Use reference books, and the school library: copy out a few lines of writing from each century to show how the language has changed.

For more information on where English words come from, see Skills Session 3, Roots (page 159).

4 Varieties of spoken English

There are lots of interesting and powerful ways of using the English language that don't follow the rules of Standard English. But unusual kinds of English – any kind of English that is different from the pronunciation, vocabulary and grammar that they were taught when they started to learn English – are going to cause problems for foreigners.

Think about the foreign visitors for whom you are preparing the School Language Guide. One thing you will need to do is explain something about all the ways of using English that they hear in your school. Some of these different kinds of English might be very different from the Standard English that they have learnt.

Accent

Where in Britain is your school? What is the local accent where you live?

Most people pronounce the sounds of words differently, depending on where in the country they come from. These different ways of pronouncing words are called **accents**. Most people's accents belong to the part of the country – the region – that they come from. So these accents are called regional accents. You can describe regional accents in different ways:

- north/south,
- Scottish/Welsh,
- Yorkshire/Lancashire,
- Scouse/Brummie,
- town/country.

Discuss the kind of regional accent that most people in your part of Britain use – try to agree about what it is usually called.

The main accent differences in England are between the north and south of the country – but every single region has an accent with special sounds. Look at the three word-maps on page 26, showing how the words *sight*, *among*, and *once* are often pronounced in different regions of England.

Try saying these words out loud yourselves, using the different sounds shown on the maps. Which is the most usual way of pronouncing each word in your region?

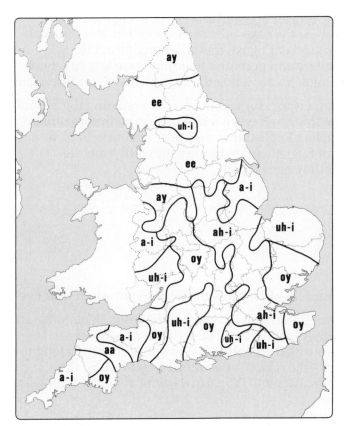

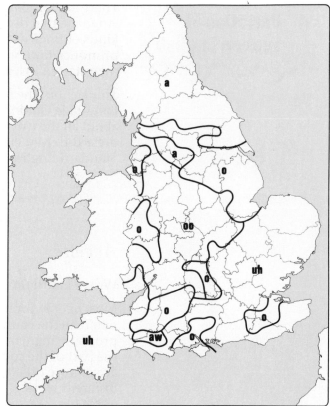

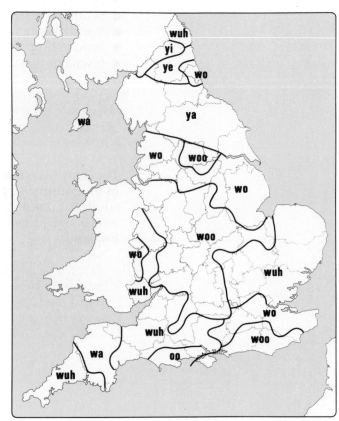

Three word maps showing how the words sight *(top left),*
among *(top right), and* once *(right) are often pronounced.*

Some people in Britain do not speak with a regional accent.

There is one accent that some people in many different parts of the country use – this is called **RP (received pronunciation)**. It is the accent used, for example, by most television and radio newsreaders. Only about 5 per cent of British people speak with this accent.

It is also the accent that foreigners usually learn – which means that they might sometimes find it difficult to understand people who live in different parts of the country.

> If you have a radio available, tune into BBC Radio 4, or Radio 3, and see if you can hear someone speaking RP. Can you think of people other than BBC newsreaders who speak with an RP accent?

It would help a foreign visitor if you could point out some of the regional and non-RP accent features that people in your school use – specially young people, who particularly like to use language in informal and unconventional ways.

> Make up sentences containing the following words (you can put more than one word in each sentence):
>
> last   sight   among   Friday   hat   bottle   isn't it?

Say each of the sentences to each other as normally as possible. Try saying them quickly and without making any special effort, and listen to how each of you pronounces these words.

Some of you will use a regional pronunciation, and some of you might use an RP pronunciation. See if you can spot how these words are pronounced in the accent of your region. See if you can spot how they are pronounced in other accents – the accents of other regions, or of RP.

> Spell out the sounds that people use in the same kind of way that is used in the word-maps.
>
> ■ Discuss and try to agree with each other whether the sounds you have heard and noted down are (1) from your region, (2) from some other region, (3) RP.
> ■ Write your findings down in your School Language Guide, under the heading: 'Local Accent Features in . . . . . . (name of your town or region)'.

Local words

Foreign visitors have more trouble with unfamiliar words than with unfamiliar accents. Some local words are very old, and often go back as far as Old English (words brought over by Angles, Saxons, Jutes and Danes). They are part of local **dialects**, and are mainly used by people whose families have lived in the region for a very long time.

All the versions of the word *silly* that are shown in this map were still being used by some people in the different regions only thirty years ago – probably at least one of these words is still being used in your region.

Some local words will confuse people from other parts of this country as much as they will confuse foreigners. Therefore, a short **glossary** of such words will be an essential part of your School Language Guide.

Glossary = a simple dictionary which explains special words used in a book (there's one in this book).

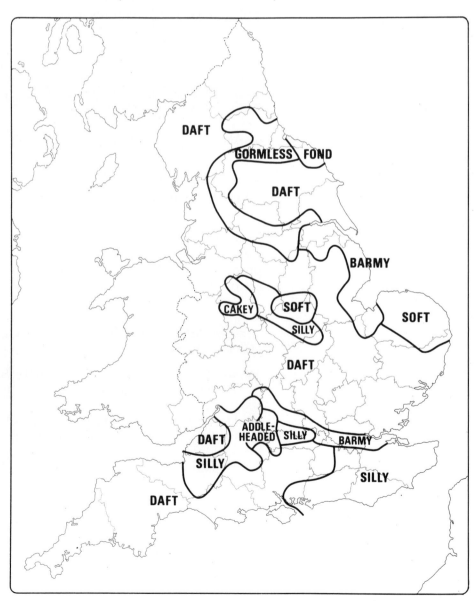

Compile a list of any unusual local words you can find and explain what they mean. These will be easier to find in some parts of the country, such as parts of the Midlands, rural England, and the north, than in others.

Do this by:

1 Class discussion. See how many local words (if any) you can think of together straight away.

2 Asking people at home – relatives and neighbours. Elderly people are likely to know more about special local words than anyone.

Of course, you might have elderly relatives living in other parts of the country – it would be interesting also to find out what they know and compare the words with the ones you find in your own region. Ask them for their expert knowledge.

Write this list by heading it 'Local words in (name of your region)' and next to each word you find, write the Standard English word for the same thing. For example:

regional   Standard English
a *sprack* child = an *active* child
leery = *hungry*

Non-standard English

Some people spend a lot of time complaining about other people who can't talk properly. What they really mean is that these people are speaking non-standard English. You have every right to use non-standard English, but it is important to know:

- what the differences are between Standard and non-standard English;
- that some people mind if you don't use Standard English on special occasions.

These are the main non-standard ways of using the English language – there aren't very many of them:

Standard English version	non-standard English version
I/ you/ we/ they like this	like*s* this
you/ we/ they were working	*was* working
isn't	*ain't*
hasn't/ haven't	*ain't*
I don't want any	I don't want *none*
she ate it quickly	she ate it *quick*
himself	his*self*
Do you see those kids?	Do you see *them* kids?
'You did that.' 'I didn't.'	'You did that.' 'I *never*.'
You're more noisy than ever. You're noisier than ever.	You're *more noisier* than ever.

Now look at the following short **transcript** of some genuine conversation – a group discussion by some secondary school third years. They don't really feel like getting on with the work they're meant to do.

Alison, Suzy, Lorna and Carole

C: I don't want to read out – who's going to read out?

A: I ain't. I don't understand anyway.

C: We got to read it all again, what she just read. I'm going to read it – no one going to read it out? Come on.

A: You read it, Carole.

C: I ain't going to read it, no way, I'm not reading out.

A: Anyway I wasn't here last time.

L: Don't matter – go on Alison.

A: Nooo.

L: Oh Alison.

A: You read it.

L: I ain't going to read it. Carole can read it

A: Oh, I'll read it then. Give us that. What's that say?

S: That's crossed out – that don't say nothing. Move, Alison!

A: I ain't got no room.

S: Alison!

A: You stop pushing.

C: I never –

A: Well –

1   You should be able to find several examples of non-standard English in that short piece. When people are having a friendly, informal conversation, they use a lot of non-standard English. Note each one down, and next to it write what the Standard English form would be.
    Discuss what's going on in this conversation – do you think they sometimes use non-standard forms for *effect*? What kind of *mood* are they in? Do you think it affects the way they use language?

2   Perform a **role play** improvisation: act out a conversation between four or five teenagers on a train, on their way into town on a Saturday afternoon – on their way to do some shopping, or to go ice-skating, or to go out for the evening. They are close friends, and talk to each other in a very informal and relaxed way.

Because they are having an informal conversation, they will probably use English in the following kinds of way:

- non-standard English;
- local words and slang;
- regional accents;
- lots of fillers (*you know, like, well, er, um, innit?, know what I mean?*)
- interrupting each other, or talking all at once;
- not explaining what they're talking about clearly (*give us that, whatsit*).

Spend some time rehearsing this, and then perform your improvisations to each other.

Listen carefully to each other's group performances – tape-record one or two if possible. Try to pick out examples of all those things in the list above of the way people use language in conversations. Note down any that you find. Discuss how realistic the different improvised conversations are.

3 Write down an imaginary version of a conversation like this, between a group of young people going out together for the day. Try to write down what they say to each other as realistically as possible, showing them using all the typical ways of speaking that often happen in conversations. Use **playscript** for this.

The difference between speech and writing

We speak as we go along – starting off in wrong directions, stopping off halfway and starting again, getting muddled and correcting ourselves, getting interrupted and forgetting what we wanted to say, pointing at things, grinning or frowning, waving our hands around, raising or lowering our voices. *Speech* is messy, and full of life.

Writing, on the other hand, is more organised – less lively, as a rule, but much clearer, much more easy to follow. When we write, we can be more in control of our words. We have the time and opportunity to wipe out our mistakes and do things again.

Look at the following two passages. They are both about the same goal being scored in the Liverpool-Roma European Cup Final of 1984. You don't have to like football to do this – in fact, you might well notice more things about how language is being used if you *don't* like football:

1 '– then forward to Johnson, Neal has gone up in support, Johnson strikes a deep cross – Whelan on the back post, beats Tancredi – and it's half clear – ball still loose (scream of 'YEAH!!' from Emlyn Hughes in the background) – and Neal has put it – into the NET!! ('HAHAHA!' from Emlyn Hughes) – and Neal scores!!!'

2 'Souness and Lee combined to send Johnston away on the right. His high centre found Tancredi fiercely challenged by Whelan at the far post and there followed a succession of Roman disasters. Tancredi dropped the ball, Bonetti tried in vain to head it behind, and then Nappi made an attempted clearance, which hit the goalkeeper. The ball rebounded to Neal and the only survivor of Liverpool's 1977 success, indeed the scorer of their third goal in that game from the penalty spot, put them ahead.'

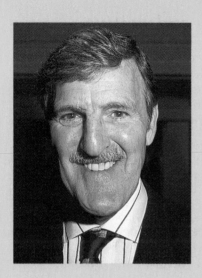

1   Discuss the differences between these two descriptions of the same goal. One of these descriptions is a written report from the *Guardian* newspaper. And one is from a BBC Radio 2 live match commentary.
It shouldn't be too hard to work out which is which – pick out as many things as you can that show which one is which.

2   Try doing some commentaries yourselves, in order to produce your own examples of speech and writing about the same thing. You will need to work together, in small groups, for this – you'll need from four to six people in each group.

■ Two or three people in each group play some simple game while the others spectate – such as: a game of snakes and ladders, a game of noughts and crosses, a game of hangman.

■ One of you provides a live commentary on the game, describing what happens as it goes on, and summing up after important moments. Another member of the group tries to note down as much of what the live commentator says, and the way it is said. Ideally this could be tape-recorded, but that is not always easy to arrange.

■ One member of the group takes notes about the game as it goes on – especially about the really good bits. This person will then write a match report after the game is over. Obviously the written report will be more detailed and organised than the live commentary.

When you have completed this, discuss the ways in which language has been used differently in the two ways of describing your big match – what are the main differences between the spoken and the written description of the match?

5 Special language for special activities

Registers

A **register** is the name for the particular way of speaking, or of writing, that *belongs* to a particular activity. It's the *special language* that goes with special activities.

Take a statement like this, for instance:

'He came out and froze. He bottled it and we had a mountain to climb after that.'

That could be someone talking quite normally and literally – perhaps about someone who is about to climb Snowdon on a very cold day, having spent all morning making home-made chutney in the open air. That makes sense – especially if it isn't an example of a particularly special way of using language.

But it makes much more sense when you see it where it belongs – as part of a short news item in a Sunday newspaper round-up of the previous day's league football games.

Ipswich's manager blamed goalkeeper Paul Cooper for the second goal, when Brazil ran onto a Perryman lob over the Ipswich defence. "He came out and froze", Ferguson said. "He bottled it and we had a mountain to climb after that."

In the language of football – the language spectators, players, managers, journalists and commentators use when talking about the game – these words and phrases have very clear meanings:

- 'he came out and froze' means that the goalkeeper couldn't decide what to do;
- 'he bottled it' means that he lost his nerve (e.g. he lost his bottle);
- 'we had a mountain to climb after that' means 'we weren't going to find it easy to win after that'.

Some people use language – special words, and ordinary words with special meanings – in this sort of way for all sorts of special activities. The people that use such language are usually *insiders* or *enthusiasts* about a particular special activity. They are part of what is going on, in the know.

The special activities with a special language – a register – of their own can be of all kinds: e.g.

music   mountaineering   horse-riding   motor mechanics   ballet dancing   angling   ice skating   religion   computers   farming and on and on . . .

The special language of each of these, and many others, serves two main purposes:

■ to describe and make the special things that go on in each activity clear – the special language helps insiders know what they're talking about;
■ to give a sense of belonging, of group membership, to the people involved in each activity – the special language sometimes closes it off to outsiders.

1   Think of a special activity that you either already know a lot about or can find out about, e.g. a sport, hobby, art-form, craft, trade or job.

The special activity that you think of could be one of the many examples already mentioned here, or it could be something else. All that matters is that it has its own special language, its own register.

Use either your own expert knowledge about that activity, the knowledge of someone who is an expert in that activity or a magazine/ newspaper that is devoted to that activity, to provide examples of the way language is used when talking or writing about it.

2 Collect together as many of the words/ phrases/ complete sentences that people involved in that activity often use when talking or writing about it, and write

EITHER

a serious, sensible and helpful glossary of the special words, the special terms, that people use – and explain what they mean – like in the following example explaining the specialist words used to name different kinds of TV programme:

game show	= a programme in which ordinary members of the public have the opportunity to appear on television, and win prizes.
soap opera	= a long-running programme telling the continuing story of a group of characters whose lives are all mixed up.
breakfast TV	= a daily magazine programme, full of news, interviews and information.
weather forecast	= a short daily programme that tells us about the following day's weather.
advertisements	= very short films to persuade us to buy things which constantly interrupt normal programmes.

OR

a humorous glossary that explains what specialist words really mean – that makes fun of the way people use words for different activities – like the examples below, which are once more about television:

game show	= a programme in which ordinary members of the public have the opportunity to be humiliated and insulted in front of millions of viewers.
soap opera	= a long-running programme full of Australians and car crashes.
breakfast TV	= a daily programme in which men in jumpers read newspapers out loud.
weather forecast	= a daily programme in which a man in a jumper uses long words to tell us what tomorrow's weather isn't actually going to be like.
advertisements	= the best things on TV, constantly interrupted by programmes.

3 Write a letter to a friend who also shares your interest and knowledge about this particular activity, telling them some news about it. Use as much of the typical language – the register – of that activity as you can.

The registers of school

Schools are full of their own special registers – special ways of talking and writing that are used for all the many different activities that go on in school. Everyone in school probably knows about these special ways of talking and writing, but they often seem mysterious to outsiders.

THE LANGUAGE REGISTERS OF DAILY SCHOOL LIFE

The language registers of daily school life do not use many specialist words. They mainly use ordinary words in special ways.

> Try to find actual, real examples of the way people use language in the following typical school situations.

1   A school assembly

Often in school assemblies, senior teachers deliver a serious and carefully prepared speech. These are sometimes a little bit like a sermon in church – using little stories to illustrate some point about good behaviour, etc. These speeches are often delivered in a very formal way.

Listen very carefully the next time this happens (if it ever does) in one of your school assemblies. Try to record some of what was said – perhaps by quickly noting down the most memorable things as soon as assembly is over.

If it was a particularly good assembly speech, you might ask the teacher who delivered it for help in this – they might have written down what they were going to say in advance, or they might have made notes.

Or, if you ask them in advance, they might let you tape-record what they say – and then you can transcribe the best bits.

2 Tellings-off

Teachers often tell pupils off – it's part of their job, and they probably get *heartily sick* of doing it. You are almost certainly very expert on the language register that teachers use to tell you off – see if you can collect and write down a few examples.

Tellings-off vary – from the *roaring angry*, or the *deeply wounded*, to the *quietly sarcastic*; from the *whole-class blast* to the *see-me-afterwards-private-chat*; from the *outright rude* to the *gently persuasive*; and lots more besides.

What kinds of language are typical of tellings-off? Although you probably know some of these by heart, real language examples need to be collected in real situations (although you must not deliberately do something wrong in order to stimulate a telling-off, please. You won't have to wait long to hear one happening on its own, probably).

Try to decide which kind of telling-off each one that you collect is. For example: *whole-class blast*.

3 Teacher talk

What sorts of things do most teachers say when they're running lessons (apart, that is, from telling you off, which is only a small part of all the talking that teachers have to do every day)?

What do different teachers say at the start of lessons, as you come in the room?

What do they say when they try to get the lesson going? Most teachers have a particular word or phrase, like 'Right then' – which they almost always say when it's time to get going.

What do they say at the end of the lesson, as you pack up and leave the room, as a rule?

4 Pupil talk

How do pupils talk when they try to answer a teacher's questions in class? What sorts of things do they say? What sorts of words, and sounds, do they use when they're not sure of an answer, when they're hesitating, when they are very keen to answer, when they're making excuses for themselves?

Present the best examples of each kind of school language that you collect as a display, and illustrate it with any suitable photos, drawings, bits of paper, that you can lay your hands on.

THE LANGUAGE REGISTERS OF DIFFERENT SUBJECTS

When you first come up to secondary school, it is often very bewildering to start spending your day moving from lesson to lesson, subject to subject. Part of the difficulty is because you have to cope with all the different ways language is used in different subjects. See if you can collect together a few examples of the different language registers of different subjects – both the things you hear and say in different subjects, and the things you read and write.

> 1   Find at least one specialist term – i.e. a word or phrase – from as many of the subjects on your timetable as you can: e.g. science, maths, CDT, cookery, PE, art, history, English, drama, RE, geography, IT, music, modern languages – or any others which you do at school.

Find these either by listening to the teacher or by looking in the textbook of a particular subject or by asking the teacher of a particular subject to give you an example of one of the specialist terms that they often use.

Every subject has its specialist terms – list examples from all of them, say what you understand them to mean, and note down whether you find them difficult to understand, or once found them difficult to understand, or never had any difficulty with them. For example:

school subject	specialist term	what it means	difficulty
English	language register	special language used for special activity	at first, not now

> 2   Collect some examples of the different language registers of different subjects by looking in your own exercise books (or folders). Find examples of three pieces of writing – one from each of three different subjects that use language in clearly and obviously different ways.

These examples might be, for instance:

■ a poem from English;
■ a write-up of an experiment in science;
■ some notes on the climate of the British Isles from geography.

Copy out enough from each – three to four lines – to show the special ways each subject uses language. Underline and comment on whatever you think is most special, or typical, of the way each subject uses language. Say whether you find it hard or easy to understand and use the special language of each of these subjects.

6 The School Language Guide

If you have worked right through this Project, you should have some – or maybe all!? – of the following kinds of language examples:

- soundbites of what people say in school;
- the way your English gets corrected in school;
- a story about how you once learnt to use language politely;
- advice to foreigners on where to find examples of Standard English;
- information about the history of the English language;
- information about the accent of your region;
- examples of special local and slang words in your school;
- information about the forms of non-standard English, and examples of them being used;
- examples of the difference between speech and writing;
- examples of different registers, both in and outside school.

Here are some suggestions for putting all this together into the School Language Guide.

REMEMBER: this Guide will provide foreigners with far more information than they can normally find about how the English language is really used in Britain.

YOU CAN PRODUCE SOMETHING GENUINELY USEFUL HERE.

1   Make a folder, with the 'School Language Guide' printed on the cover.

2   Rearrange all the material you have under the following (suggested) headings:

- 'The Way People Talk in School': including soundbites, school conversations, local and slang words, the language registers of school, the accents of your school.
- 'Learning English': including how you first learned about using language politely, what English teachers teach, the history of Standard English, the forms of Standard and non-standard English, the differences between speech and writing.

3   Prepare a full contents list.

4   Write an introduction for anyone who uses this in the future, telling them what they will find in your Language Guide. Explain about all the different kinds of English that they will find inside the Guide – explain how they are different, and why we like to use English in all these different ways.

telling stories

Contents

Introduction

You already know a lot about telling stories. You've probably told quite a few yourself, in one way and another.

This Project aims to show you some ways of thinking about telling stories, that can help you write even more, and even better stories than before. It will help you think about some of the reasons for writing stories, some of the ways of making them enjoyable, and some of the different kinds of stories you can write.

If you practise these, you'll find yourself asking some useful questions about how to write stories. The main aim of this Project is to leave you with these questions – and to let you find new answers every time you write a new story.

Products

You should end up with all kinds of different stories, which you've enjoyed writing and other people will enjoy reading.

Audience

It's no good writing a story if no one reads it. You'll be writing stories for real readers – different stories for different readers, of all ages.

1 Telling tall stories

A good tall story should:

■ start off sounding *completely believable*,
■ end up as obviously *quite incredible*.

Sometimes people make up really clever stories when they need an excuse for something. The most successful excuses are usually very simple, but really imaginative ones are more entertaining:

"My mother used my exercise book to light the fire, I'm afraid."
"The cat was sick over it, miss."
"The school bus was hijacked by Lithuanian terrorists, sir."

These might not be very believable, but at least they're enjoyable.

Tell a really enjoyable tall story as an excuse for either arriving late at school, or not giving in your homework.

First of all, write your tall story. Use no more than a side of paper, and write it in three paragraphs.

PARAGRAPH ONE

This opening paragraph should be entirely believable, down-to-earth, and convincing. Fill it with everyday details that will convince the reader to trust in the *truth* of the story. For example:

> I set off for school at my normal time this morning. I waved hello to the milkman while I pumped up the front tyre on my bike, which was just a little bit flat. I went back inside to pick up my homework, which I nearly forgot, and then I set off. I was still on good time as I cycled up Filbert Street, and got to the crossroads with Chester Avenue.

PARAGRAPH TWO

This middle paragraph should look quite normal at first, but you ought to drop in one or two details that are unusual, just to get the reader ready for what's coming next:

> It took a long time to cross Chester Avenue, there was so much traffic. I had to wait ages for three buses, a car transporter and an elephant to go by. I was beginning to get a bit late already, and I knew I'd better get a move on if I was not going to get into trouble. I'm always very careful not to get into trouble, as everyone knows.

PARAGRAPH THREE

This final paragraph is when you really let the reader have it. This is when you let your story take off:

> As I was cycling up Chester Avenue, as fast as I could go, a lady in blue overalls and a peaked cap waved me down and asked me if I'd seen her elephant anywhere. I told her where it had gone, and she asked me to show her. We found the elephant sitting in someone's front garden, eating their daffodils. It seemed pleased to see us. The lady explained that this elephant had an odd taste in music, and did I happen to know anything by The Wedding Present? I certainly *did*. Before I knew what was happening, I'd been hoisted up onto the elephant's back and I was whistling into this elephant's ear, while the lady led us back to the private zoo that it had escaped from. It was right over the other side of town, and that's why I'm so late, you see.

 When you've written your *un*believable tall story as *believably* as you can, try telling it to someone with as much conviction as you can, as if it was completely true, like you believe every word of it. Have a competition to see who can come up with the most *convincing* and *tallest* story of all.

2 Stories for very young children

- What kinds of stories do very young children (aged two to four) enjoy?
- What sorts of characters and events should you put into stories for very young children?
- What sort of words do you need to use for very young children, and how should you design books for them?

What stories do young children enjoy?

What kinds of stories did you enjoy when you were very young?

> Talk about the very first books or stories you can remember enjoying. Which one did you like best? Which bits did you like best?

If you still have any of your earliest books at home, bring one or two in, and read out your favourite bits to each other.

What kinds of stories for children on TV did you most enjoy when you first watched TV? What were they about: machines? animals? humans?

Talk about the kinds of stories that very young children seem to enjoy. Are they interested in finding out what happens in a story, or do they just enjoy what they see in the pictures? Can they even follow real stories?

Look at the short extracts (on pages 46–47) from books popular with the two to four age group.

> Discuss and note down in rough your answers to the following questions:
>
> - What different kinds of main character seem to appeal to readers in this particular age group?
> - What kinds of event seem to interest them?

How was school, Spot?

Okay.

"It's bathtime, Jack," called Dad.
"I hate baths!" said Jack.

"That's all right, Thomas. You made me laugh. I like that. I'm in disgrace," Gordon went on pathetically, "I feel very low."

"I'm in disgrace too," said Thomas.

"Why! so you are Thomas; we're both in disgrace. Shall we form an Alliance?"

"An Ally – what – was – it?"

"An Alliance, Thomas, 'United we stand, together we fall,'" said Gordon grandly.

"You help me, and I help you. How about it?"

"Right you are," said Thomas.

"Good! That's settled," rumbled Gordon.

And buffer to buffer the Allies puffed home.

48

"It's a real scorcher to-day," said Pat to Jess, as they drove along. "Phew, I'm thirsty already."
The lakes were drying up. The stream was down to a trickle.

These four examples show you the four kinds of stories that pre-school children usually enjoy:

1 Stories about animals – usually furry, loveable animals like dogs, cats, small bears, etc. Often these animals talk and have human-type adventures.

2 Stories about children – for very young children, such stories often show things that very young children know most about, e.g. stories about home, going on holiday, going shopping, playing with animals, etc.

3 Stories about machines – like trains, cars, helicopters, with human faces and characters.

4 Stories about people who do special jobs – like bus-drivers, firefighters, farmers, sailors, etc. – that interest very young children. Children often like to play with toys that reflect these jobs.

Carry out a survey of books for very young children, including ones you used to enjoy a lot, and collect information that you can fill onto a chart like the one below.

name of book	intended age	main character	events in story	sample sentence

Writing books for the very young

Now that you know something about the books that young children like, you can try to write one yourself.

Books for very young children should not be very long. The stories need to be clear and simple, and the language should not be too complicated.

Most importantly, these books will need to:

■ be about the things these children enjoy – about things they can understand, and about the kinds of characters they usually like;
■ be entertaining – that is: funny, surprising, original.

They certainly need to be illustrated, but if you can't produce brilliant drawings that doesn't matter. Many successful children's books have very simple illustrations – even matchstick people would be better than nothing.

1   Invent a main character, for example:

■ animal – *Gary the Gerbil*
■ child – *Karen Kareless*
■ machine – *Trevor the Trashvan*
■ adult – *Spacewoman Stella*

2   Try out some ideas for simple things that can happen to this character, and discuss them with each other:

■ Will very young children like the character?
■ Will they understand the story, and the words you use?
■ Will it make them laugh?

3   Make your finished version look good – use colour, and keep it simple. Take your finished version to a playgroup if you can, so that you can watch what happens when the children look at it for themselves, or when you actually read it to them.

 It would feel GREAT if you knew that, one day, some very young child wanted to hear your book again because that was their favourite.

3 Making stories believable

Why do we believe in impossible things?

In Walt Disney's *Dumbo*, a baby elephant with large ears learns to fly.
In *The BFG*, a friendly giant collects dreams with a butterfly net.
In *Dr Who*, a scatty scientist travels through time in a police telephone box.

None of these stories are about things that are possible in the real world, but that doesn't stop us from enjoying them. A story can be told in animated drawings, in books, or on TV with cut-price special effects: but we can still *believe* in it enough to enjoy it, and enough to *care about what happens*. Why?

Human beings like stories so much that they're ready to believe in anything, however unlikely, if it's told in a convincing way. A story doesn't have to be absolutely possible in real-life to be believable. It can be completely impossible, in fact, so long as:

- we believe in the characters, they have thoughts and feelings like our own, and we care about what happens to them;
- the story is told as if it was true and possible.

> Discuss what makes stories believable.
> Choose three stories that you all know:
>
> - a film – like an *Indiana Jones* or a *James Bond* story;
> - a book – like *The BFG* or *Freaky Friday;*
> - a TV drama – like *Neighbours* or *Casualty.*

On your own, first of all, take each one that you have chosen in turn, and give it marks out of 5 (0 = not at all . . . 5 = very much) for each of the following things:

1   Does the story work for you? Do you find it convincing? Do you care about what happens?

2   Could this story happen in real-life?

3   Are any of the characters attractive? Do you like any of the characters?

4   Are the things the characters say, and feel, and do, believable?

5   Are the small details of how the story is told convincing? If, for example, there's a flying elephant in the story, does it seem to fly in the way you'd expect an elephant to fly?

Discuss the marks that each of you give to each of the three stories for these five questions (top mark would be 25), and talk about your reasons for your decisions. Try to decide what it is about the different stories that makes you either believe, or not believe, in them.

Story-telling is like acting

Actors are like story-tellers. They have to make impossible things seem convincing all the time. Good actors make you believe that they really are someone they're not.

Even if the story they're acting is completely impossible in real-life,

- if they act as though it was real;
- if they act as if they really were the character they're playing:
- if they take care to make the small details of their performance true-to-life;

then audiences believe in the characters they're playing, and care about what happens to them.

> Try a simple experiment. Act out a well-known children's story, like *Goldilocks and the Three Bears*, *Little Red Riding Hood*, or *The Three Little Pigs*. Act it as convincingly and realistically as possible.

For instance, in *Goldilocks*, you would need to make the three bears very human in their behaviour (in a bear-like way, of course). If they came back to their house and found signs of an intruder, they'd be nervous and angry and confused. What would they say, what emotions would show on their faces, how would they move?

And what about Goldilocks? What kind of person wanders into a strange house and starts eating porridge? Would she be a sweet little girl, or rather a careless, or silly, or wild, or selfish person?

1   Talk about whichever story you choose before you start.

2   Think about how the characters ought to act, and react to each other, in order to be convincing.

3   Think about the details of their behaviour, the little things that people might do in such a situation.

4   Above all, think about how you'd convince an audience that this story was *really happening*, so that they cared about the characters, and wanted to know the ending.

Rehearse it carefully, and then act out your version to an audience – probably the rest of the class. Discuss the things in each other's performances that either succeeded or failed to make people believe in the story while it was going on.

Making your own story believable – part one

FIRST DRAFT

Write the **first draft** of a story about a twelve year old child who has discovered the magic power of turning into a thirty year old adult for just ten minutes a day, whenever that can help her get out of trouble, or rescue someone else from difficulties.

You don't need to explain the whole history of how the child discovers this power – just tell one incident of her or him using this power.

In this first draft, you just need to work out what happens in the story – it might be something funny, or frightening, or brave. Think about your main character – the child with this amazing power – and decide where she or he is going to use it: at home? at school? in a supermarket?

Then write your first version of the story as quickly as possible.

How the experts make stories believable

If you are telling a story for someone to read, or out loud to an audience, you need to think about the same basic question: How do you make people *believe* in the story, so that they *care* about what happens to the characters?

When you're telling a story – either writing it or speaking it – you have a great advantage: you can use your role as story-teller to convince people it's true.

Look at these three extracts from popular stories.

1   The first extract is from *Under Plum Lake* by Lionel Davidson. This is a fantasy tale, and in this extract Barry, who is telling the story, is being shown what power tobogganing is like. They use power from the mountain itself, which is of course completely impossible in real-life.

He started off fast right away, and he didn't even bother putting power on at the first wide bend, just yelled, 'Right!' and I swung out and we lurched round the bend at speed. I felt my heart beginning to thud. I could see the red sign ahead for a hairpin bend. It came rushing up in a sickening blur, and he still didn't put power on. He began yelling, '*Left! Left!*' without slackening speed for an instant. I saw, without believing it, that he didn't mean to put power on at all. We were going racing into the hairpin bend. He was leaning out to left himself. I leaned out as far as I could. I leaned so far my head brushed the snow on the banking as we swished in a jackknife curve round it, and levelled out into a wild dangerous wobble, racing from side to side of the icy track as he hurtled down it, not losing speed for an instant.

2   The second extract is from *The BFG* by Roald Dahl. A little girl called Sophie has just been kidnapped by the Big Friendly Giant, who is telling her about all the amazing things he can do:

'I can hear plants and trees.'
'Do *they* talk?' Sophie asked.
'They is not exactly talking,' the BFG said. 'But they is making noises. For instance, if I come along and I is picking a lovely flower, if I is twisting the stem of the flower till it breaks, then the plant is screaming. I can hear it screaming and screaming very clear.'
'You don't mean it!' Sophie cried. 'How awful!'
'It is screaming just like you would be screaming if someone was twisting *your* arm right off.'
'Is that really true?' Sophie asked.
'You think I is swizzfiggling you?'
'It *is* rather hard to believe.'
'Then I is stopping right here,' said the BFG sharply. 'I is not wishing to be called a fibster.'
'Oh no! I'm not calling you anything!' Sophie cried. 'I believe you! I do really! Please go on!'
   The BFG gave her a long hard stare. Sophie looked right back at him, her face open to his. 'I believe you,' she said softly.

3 The third extract is from a story called *My Friend Mr Leakey* by J.B.S. Haldane. The person telling the story describes various adventures with a magician, such as the time the magician made them both invisible in order to turn a vicious dog's teeth into rubber.

When we went round the street corner we became visible again, which was rather a relief to me, because it is certainly odd to feel bits of oneself without seeing them. As we got into another taxi, Mr Leakey said, 'If that man had any sense, which he hasn't, he'd make a fortune by showing Fido at fairs as The Rubber-Toothed Dog, and charging people sixpence to let him bite them.' By the way, if anyone who reads this does see a rubber-toothed dog at a fair, I wish they'd write to me, because I should like to meet Fido again, and see if he's got accustomed to his rubber teeth, like people get accustomed to false ones.

These three story-tellers all take great care to make you believe in their stories. They use various story-telling *tricks*.

- They describe details very realistically.
- The characters have real human feelings.
- The story-teller – the **narrator** – talks as if the tale was completely true.

Discuss each extract in turn, and talk about the different methods each author uses to do those things.

Making your own story believable – part two

SECOND DRAFT

The *way* you tell a story is as important as *what happens*. Once you've thought of interesting and exciting things that can happen in your story, you can concentrate on finding ways of making readers believe in what you've made up, so that they want to read the whole thing.

Write a **second draft** of your story about the child who can turn into a thirty year old adult, and this time take great care to:

- make the details convincing, especially the unbelievable bits;
- make the characters act, speak and feel like real people;
- tell it as if it was absolutely true (as if *you* believed in it completely). You could tell it in the **first person**, as if you were part of the story, or in the **third person**, as if you were reporting something you had heard about that had happened to other people.

If you are having difficulty with punctuation,
turn to Skills Session 5 on page 162.

4 Different types of stories for different readers

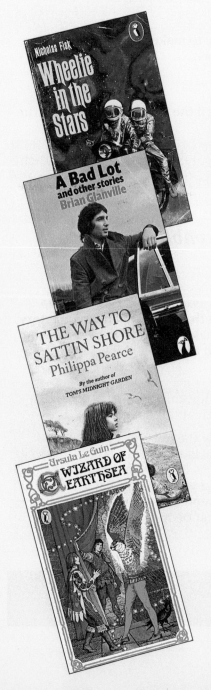

What do you like in a story?

If you looked at the **blurb** on the back of a *western* book, or a *romance*, you might be able to spot some typical ingredients like these:

westerns	romances
cowboys	handsome doctors
saloon bars	nervous nurses
horses	heartbreak
good guys	sunsets
bad guys	misunderstandings
wild frontiers	tears
shoot-outs	kisses
rough justice	marriage

Here are extracts from the publisher's blurbs on the back covers of four different books by well-known children's authors.

What typical ingredients can you spot in these four extracts?
What other ingredients might you expect to find in each of these books?

1 Life as cargostrippers on Terramare 3 was boring and ugly. Even so, it seemed crazy for Noll and Niven to dream about driving their beautiful smuggled-in motorbike, Wheelie. Machines that ran on petrol were banned nowadays, but Noll and Niven would not give up. 'Something will happen, somehow, sometime,' Noll said, and indeed it did, though it was rather more than they had bargained for.

2 Football and boxing are two of the toughest and most competitive sports and footballers and boxers amongst the highest-paid professionals. The rewards and temptations are enormous, the pressures intense. 'Neither is a game for lasses. If they kick you, kick 'em back.'

3 'At the moment of disappointment – of a kind of explosive despair – the idea came into Kate's head that she would visit Sattin Shore . . . she would go there by herself, tomorrow.'
   There is a mystery about Kate's family, but her family either knows nothing or will tell nothing. Her two elder brothers, her grandmother, her new friend Anna and her missing father all have a part to play in Kate's search to fit the jigsaw pieces of past and present to find a new picture for the future.

4 A tale of wizards, dragons and terrifying shadows.
   The young wizard Sparrowhawk, tempted by pride to try spells beyond his powers, lets loose an evil shadow-beast in his land. Only he can destroy it, and this quest leads him to the farthest corner of Earthsea.

1 Write your own lists of the ingredients you can spot in each of these blurbs, that show you what kind of book each one probably is. Also write down any other typical ingredients that you think belong in each kind of book.

2 Do any of these four books appeal to you? Try to describe the different sorts of reader who would probably like each of these books in turn.

3 Write the blurb that you might find on the back cover of either a western or a romance.
You don't need to write an actual book first, though – just think of the kind of story you'd find in either a typical western or a typical romance, and make up the names of the main characters, and decide where it could take place (the **setting**).

If you are choosing a book to read, you probably read the blurb written on the cover.

■ What ingredients usually appeal to *you*?
■ What ingredients usually put *you* off reading a book?

Write these down in a chart like this:

appealing ingredients	off-putting ingredients

4 Carry out a class survey of what stories are most popular. You might find that there are two or three different kinds of book that most people like to read, or maybe more.

Get together with any people who like the same kinds of story ingredients as you, and produce your own top ten story ingredients – the ingredients you most hope to find in the stories you like to read.

5 Make a big chart of these, and also write down the names of any books that you think are particularly good examples of your favourite kinds of books. Stick this up on the wall, and encourage your teacher or librarian to look at what you say – perhaps they'll be able to get hold of more books like that.

What do nine year olds like to read?

When Eric Stanley Pigeon's eyes opened, the first thing upon which they focused was a sheet of newpaper. Mrs Pigeon had not bothered with much of a nest, but she had decorated the site with a few oddments picked up from the pavement below – a cigarette packet, some milk-bottle tops, a sweet-wrapper and a piece of newspaper. Thus it was that Eric Stanley Pigeon's first experience of the printed word came in the shape of the racing page of *The Daily Echo*, informing him of the runners and riders for the meetings at Redcar and Uttoxeter, six weeks earlier.

Something about the lists of horses seemed to attract Eric Stanley Pigeon, and he began to peck vigorously at one particular name.

'Leave that alone, Eric Stanley!' said Mrs Pigeon sharply. 'You don't known where it's been.

(from *E.S.P.* by Dick King-Smith)

The Horse had lifted its head. Shasta stroked its smooth-as-satin nose and said, 'I wish *you* could talk, old fellow.'

And then for a second he thought he was dreaming, for quite distinctly, though in a low voice, the Horse said, 'But I can.'

Shasta stared into its great eyes and his own grew almost as big, with astonishment. 'How ever did *you* learn to talk?' he asked.

'Hush! Not so loud,' replied the Horse. 'Where I come from, nearly all the animals talk.'

(from *The Horse and his Boy* by C.S. Lewis)

Both these writers are very popular with children in the eight to ten age range. These extracts should give you some clues about what children of that age like to find in the stories they read.

What ingredients did you notice in each story? In one story there's a young pigeon who can predict the winners of horse-races. The pigeon has a funny name, it can do amazing things, and its mother talks English. In the second story there's a talking horse, and the way the boy Shasta discovers he can talk is described humorously.

There are three things in both these stories that are typical of many of the books that children of this age like to read:

- animals
- magic
- humour

Of course, you can find other kinds of books that are popular with this age range – books about school, about space-travel, about real-life adventure – but if it turns out to be true that children of this age particularly like stories about animals, magic and humour, then that might be a good formula to use when you write a story for children of that age.

You are going to write a story which you either give primary school pupils in the eight to ten years age range to read on their own, or which you are going to read out loud, or tell them.
You are going to test out whether animals, magic and humour make a good formula to use for stories for children of that age.

STAGE ONE: FIRST DRAFT

Have a first try at writing a story for eight to ten year olds with animals, magic and humour in it. The two most important things are:

1   to write something that you enjoy and find entertaining;

2   to write something that the people who are meant to read your story will understand and enjoy.

You choose exactly how you're going to use these different story ingredients.

- Is there a particular kind of animal (or bird, or fish!) that you know a lot about, or that you particularly like?
- Think of something particularly clever that this animal can be made to do: talk? ride a bike? have secret adventures? stop humans from doing stupid things?
- You could invent a child of the same age as the children you're writing for, who knows all about what this animal can do, and tries to hide that from grown-ups. The story could be about a time when the animal's secret is nearly found out.

You must choose what happens – *keep it simple*, because you are writing for younger children – and full of *fun*.

Your first draft is for working out what happens. Stories don't usually come out exactly right the first time you write them – don't worry about making it perfect. Write a first draft, and then give it to someone else in the class to read.

Discuss with each other whether you've got the ingredients right, and how you think younger readers will feel about what each of you has written. Listen to each other's advice, and make any changes which seem helpful.

STAGE TWO: TRYING OUT YOUR STORY

First of all, read your stories to one or two younger children, or give them the stories to read on their own. This means going to a primary school, or using younger sisters, brothers or neighbours.

If you can, watch them carefully while you read the story to them, or while they read it to themselves. Watch their reactions:

- Do they lose interest at any point?
- Do they laugh at some bits? (and are they bits they were meant to laugh at?)
- Are they keen to know the ending?

Afterwards, talk to the children if you can, and ask them questions like this:

- Was it the kind of story you like?
- Did you find it easy to follow what was going on in the story?
- Was the ending good?
- Would you like to read another story like this?
- What didn't you like about the story?
- Were there bits you couldn't understand? Were there words you couldn't understand?

Give them a real chance to let you know about bits they didn't like, and bits they did like.

STAGE THREE: FINAL VERSION

In class, discuss how your stories worked, and what you learnt about what your audience/readers liked and didn't like.

Discuss with each other how you can improve your stories – and then work on the changes you think are necessary.

You might want to test them out again: in which case, go through Stage Two a second time.

Finish by making an **anthology** out of all your finished stories and present it to a primary school. Ask the teachers and pupils to let you know how it goes down with its readers over the coming months.

5 People tell stories for different reasons

Newspapers tell stories

Newspapers tell big, important stories – about things like wars, and earthquakes, and accidents, and elections. They also tell small, trivial, gossipy stories – those are the kinds of stories that people seem to like best. For instance:

Boy brings plane down

A TEENAGER took over and landed a plane after the pilot collapsed at the controls. Peter Spalding, 19, brought the Normad turbo-prop aircraft down with radio instructions.

An Australian Aviation Department spokesman said Peter, from Melbourne, landed at Broken Hill airport 380 miles west of Canberra.

Help! A tot in the pot

Saucy tot Juliana Taw landed in a right old fix when she became wedged in the loo seat with her head down the pan!

Mum Girda, 34, struggled frantically, but couldn't free the two-year-old at their home in Reginald Road, Scunthorpe, Humberside.

Six firemen and an ambulance crew couldn't free her either, until they SAWED through the plastic seat.

A fireman said: "Despite her predicament she thought it was a huge joke."

What things in these two stories are typical of the way stories are told in newspapers? What details do the stories include, what language do they use, that show you that these are newspaper stories?

Think of some very minor event that you heard about recently:

- someone falling off their bike,
- someone getting put in detention,
- someone's television breaking down.

Write a short news story, using newspaper methods of telling a story

- giving lots of factual information,
- quoting what people said,
- using newspaper language,
- telling the story very briefly,

and turning it into either a funny, or dramatic, news story.

Look through several newspapers, and see if you can find any other stories like these – very short stories about odd events, some silly, some funny, some genuinely dramatic or sad. Make a wall-poster made up entirely of these news-stories, and see which ones people enjoy reading most. Why do people like reading these odd little stories?

There is also help available on page 164:
Skills Session 6, How to write tabloid news stories.

Stories can be used to sell things

Some advertisements just *show* people happily using a product – cats happily eating cat food, children happily eating beans, people happily driving cars, or washing their hair, or their clothes – then they just *tell* you how good it is.

But sometimes advertisements tell very short stories that illustrate how useful, enjoyable, or smart, a product is and that the kind of people who use this product are always doing things that are fun, or smart, or exciting. For example:

- the man and woman who begin to fall in love over endless cups of instant coffee;
- Michael J. Fox risking his life to fetch a can of cola for his new female neighbour;
- the man and woman who have a row outside a nightclub. She slaps him and goes inside. He sends her some expensive chocolates, which shows what a nice man he is – they kiss and make up.

Talk about any adverts you can remember that tell stories, and note down what happened in each advert and, if you can, spend an evening watching the latest television adverts and note down what happens in any adverts that tell a story.

Discuss why you think the advertisers chose to tell each particular story. For instance: stories in advertisements often show some *problem* happening that is *solved* by the particular product that is being advertised. Or the story might just be something funny, or cheerful, that presents the product in a pleasant, good-humoured way. Or it might be dramatic, so that the product itself seems to be something exciting.

Write a story that advertises one of the following kinds of product: perfume or aftershave, a dishwasher, sunglasses, alcohol-free lager. Tell the story like a modern fairy tale, beginning 'Once upon a time . . .' For example:

Once upon a time there was a young person called Bernard. He was a nice boy, and he used to take his dog, Bouncer, for a walk through the town centre every evening. Bernard always smiled at everyone he met, he was kind to his dog, and was never boastful.

The other young people used to laugh at Bernard. They said he wasn't tough, and he wasn't cool. The other boys would lounge around at street corners as Bernard went by, and call him names. The girls would point him out to each other and giggle. This made Bernard unhappy.

One day, Bernard's very smart aunt Melissa gave him a pair of **raybang!** sunglasses for his birthday. These are the coolest, toughest sunglasses in the world.

That evening when Bernard took Bouncer out for a walk, no one laughed at him. No one called him names, or giggled. When Bernard walked by, all the girls followed him.

When he and Bouncer went into the park, so did the girls. When Bernard threw a piece of wood into the lake for Bouncer, all the girls dived in to fetch it. Bernard just looked at them, splashing around and fighting over the piece of wood, and grinned quietly. He touched his **raybang!** dark sunglasses for a moment, and walked off into the sunset with Bouncer, looking like the coolest, toughest boy in the world.

Whichever way you tell it, this story will need to be very short, and entertaining. And it should make the reader like the product.

Stories can tell you how to behave

MORAL LESSONS

Every religion uses simple stories to explain things to people about what to believe and about how to behave.

Children's stories have often been used to teach moral lessons, especially in the past – lessons about life, and how to behave well. Stories like *The Boy Who Cried Wolf*, *The Tortoise and the Hare*, and *The Three Little Pigs* are very simple attempts to teach young children how to live properly.

The story of *The Three Little Pigs* is very instructive. Three youngsters set off from their mother's home, to make a life for themselves. Two of them are too careless and lazy to build a solid and safe life for themselves – one makes a house of straw, and the other makes a house of sticks. The big

Here is the big bad wolf.

He looks at the little pig
in the house of straw.

I can get that little pig,
he says.

26   27

bad wolf – who is everything *dangerous and wicked* out in the big bad world – gets them. But he can't do a thing about the young pig who goes to the trouble to make a house of bricks. The pig who works hard, and prepares for the future, beats the big bad wolf. The message is clear: *you'd better work hard and live sensibly, or you'll end up in big trouble.*

Of course, you could tell any of these stories to give a very different kind of message. For instance, you could tell the story of *The Three Little Pigs* to show how boring life is if you always play safe, like the third pig who settled down in his brick house. The pig in the straw house could be shown nipping out the back when the wolf comes, and going off somewhere else and having a really exciting life. The pig in the stick house could invite the wolf in for a beer, and then discover what an interesting bloke the wolf really is. They become the best of friends, and have a good laugh at the pig in the brick house, sitting there worrying all the time.

> Re-tell an old children's story with a moral lesson, and have some fun with it. Turn the lesson on its head, and find a way of teaching children something very different from what was originally intended.

You could do this with *The Boy Who Cried Wolf*, or *The Tortoise and the Hare*, or any other story of this kind that you know well.

HIDDEN MESSAGES

Some stories are used to give sensible advice. These are sometimes a little boring, because the best stories are seldom sensible.

The advice in this story is very sensible – and if children do enjoy reading it, then they will certainly learn useful things along the way.

Topsy and Tim TAKE NO RISKS gives more than one message, in fact. Although it seems to be telling children the simple message that they must be careful about certain things, like weed-killer in the garden shed and bleach in the kitchen, it also gives another very different kind of message. Look at the extract from the book on the next page.

Uncle Frank and Aunt Doris actually live together in the same house, although it's hard to believe it from that extract. Why is it Uncle Frank's garden, and Aunt Doris's house, exactly? This book is giving us the message that *housework is women's business* and that *men leave that kind of stuff to the women.* The book tells children that this is what's *normal.* The message might not have been intended, but it's there anyway.

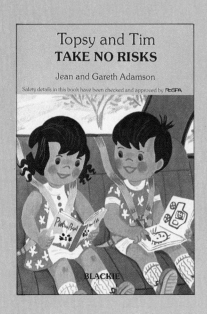

Stories are full of messages like this – hidden messages about what is normal in life. And that's how we really learn about the world. Messages like this don't only happen in stories for children. You can find them in many of the programmes you watch on television, in advertisements, in magazines and in newspapers. Every time you switch on the television, or read something, messages about what is meant to be normal (about how women, men, children, or old people should behave) are hidden in the stories we enjoy.

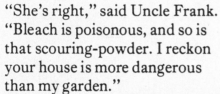

"She's right," said Uncle Frank. "Bleach is poisonous, and so is that scouring-powder. I reckon your house is more dangerous than my garden."

Aunt Doris looked a tiny bit pink and cross. She put the bottle of bleach and the scouring-powder away safely in a cupboard.

⑦ Choose one children's television programme that you all know well, and watch it carefully. Discuss any hidden messages that you can find in it, about the way children, men, women, or old people should normally behave.

6 Thinking about stories

Sometimes you get stuck when writing a story. You are not sure what to do next or what has gone wrong. This last section of this Project should help you by showing you different ways of thinking about stories.

What is a story?

Stories begin by letting you know something about where the story is taking place, and by introducing you to some characters. They tell you a bit about the characters, and maybe even get you interested in finding out more about them. But all the time, as you begin to get interested in a story, you're asking yourself: *'What's going to happen?'*

Sometimes big things, or terrible things, happen to the characters. Sometimes something quite ordinary happens.
But if nothing happens at all, you're going to think to yourself: 'That was a pretty rotten story. Nothing happened.'

The most important question you need to answer when you're writing a story, is: *'What's going to happen in this story?'*

Why tell stories?

Stories can be used to:

- entertain us,
- teach us things,
- persuade us to do things,
- persuade us not to do things,
- give us information,
- tell us what the world is really like,
- help us forget what the world is really like, for a while.

When you start to write a story, you should ask yourself why you are writing it:

- Is this just for fun?
- Is there something I've got to tell people about?
- What do I want the people who read this to get from the story?

All stories need to be entertaining. But stories are sometimes not just for entertainment – sometimes people tell stories for special reasons and purposes, for example:

- when they're making *excuses* for things they've done,
- telling us *news* about something that's happened,
- trying to *persuade* us to do something,
- trying to *influence* us in some way.

A children's story entirely in pictures

What about the readers?

Think about who is going to read your story, and about the kinds of thing they will enjoy reading. Decide what type of story to tell, and choose the story ingredients to put into it.

Make your readers read your story in whatever way you want:

- you can decide to make them laugh, or to make them feel sad,
- you can make them like or dislike characters in the story, and
- you can choose when to keep the readers in suspense.

You're in charge of how people read your stories. Ask yourself: *'What do I want the readers to be thinking right now?'*

See Skills Session 7, Controlling readers' expectations, page 166.

How do you tell stories?

You can tell a story in lots of ways:

- like it really happened to you, and you're part of the story;
- like it was just something that happened to other people – as if you were just a reporter, passing on the facts to the readers;
- like it was something amazing or funny or terrible that happened to these people you know everything about – and as if you, the story-teller, know exactly what goes on in the characters' minds. You're in charge of the story, and you know everything about it.

Each time you tell a story, think about the kind of story-teller you're going to be, this time.

The picture at the top of the next page collects together all the different ways of thinking about stories that are in this Project. The next few times you write a story of your own, and it's not going very well, keep asking yourself the questions on this chart as you go along – they will help you make your mind up about what you want to do:

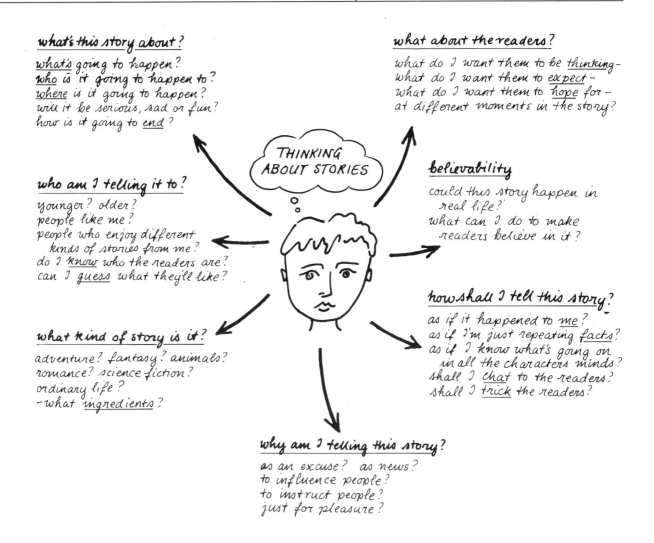

what's this story about?

what's going to happen?
who is it going to happen to?
where is it going to happen?
will it be serious, sad or fun?
how is it going to end?

what about the readers?

what do I want them to be thinking—
what do I want them to expect—
what do I want them to hope for—
at different moments in the story?

who am I telling it to?

younger? older?
people like me?
people who enjoy different
   kinds of stories from me?
do I know who the readers are?
can I guess what they'll like?

THINKING ABOUT STORIES

believability

could this story happen in
   real life?
what can I do to make
   readers believe in it?

what kind of story is it?

adventure? fantasy? animals?
romance? science fiction?
ordinary life?
—what ingredients?

how shall I tell this story?

as if it happened to me?
as if I'm just repeating facts?
as if I know what's going on
   in all the characters minds?
shall I chat to the readers?
shall I trick the readers?

why am I telling this story?

as an excuse? as news?
to influence people?
to instruct people?
just for pleasure?

The Great Escape, which is a children's story, is told entirely in pictures. There is a sample page from *The Great Escape* on page 65. This page shows just one adventure out of many that happen to the hero, an escaped prisoner unsuccessfully pursued throughout the book by some exhausted prison guards.

As a final exercise in this Project, see how differently one story can look, if you make different decisions about how to write it.
Write short versions of the story *The Great Escape* in each of these ways:

■ a short **news item** in a paper, or on the radio news: giving the facts in a lively and entertaining way;
■ an **advertisement**: using the story to make some product look good;
■ a **first person narrative**: in other words, tell the story as if you were the escaped convict;
■ a **third person narrative**: in other words, the story is happening to other people, not you. You tell the readers what all the characters are thinking about;
■ a **moral tale**: you tell the story as a warning against bad behaviour. The story's moral is that one mustn't break the law.

managing information

Contents

Introduction

However much you know, you can't possibly keep every single detailed piece of information you might need stored away in your head. Today, when the amount of information available is far greater than at any time in history, it's important that you know how to get hold of, and interpret, different kinds of information.

In this Project you'll have the opportunity to find out how to track down, make sense of, and convey all kinds of information. You'll have the chance to learn how to *use* information so that you can become more independent both in your daily life and in your learning in school.

Products

You'll be producing leaflets, brochures and information sheets. The final product will be an investigation and report about the World of Books.

Audience

Some of the material you produce will be for you and other people in your class; some will be for parents or guardians and visitors to your school.

1 Information is everywhere

In pairs, discuss how you would try to find the answers to the questions below. Where would you go? Who would you ask? Decide *how* you would find the answers.

1 How far is Venus from Earth?

2 How do you use a payphone?

3 What lessons do the fifth years have on Friday afternoons?

4 How long does it take to cook a jacket potato in a microwave oven?

5 What's in a Mars Bar?

6 Is there a direct train from Manchester to London on Saturday mornings?

7 Who won the women's tennis singles at Wimbledon in 1989?

8 What's on television this evening?

9 Who wrote *David Copperfield*?

10 How do you treat a wasp-sting?

11 What is Jane Goodall famous for?

12 Is it likely to rain tomorrow?

13 Why were Egyptian mummies covered in bandages?

14 Is there a motorway from Leeds to Edinburgh?

15 What does 'regurgitation' mean?

Choose three questions each and find the answers.

HAMPSHIRE COUNTY LIBRARY

CHILDREN'S GUIDE

WHO CAN JOIN?

YOU CAN!!

Using the library

1 In pairs or small groups, draw up a list of how you use libraries. For example, if you have been to the school library recently for private study and to use reference books, write down:

> School library – reference books
> – private study

If you use a public library, add that to your list. For example:

> Local public library – borrow a book about gerbils

Decide who is going to report back to the rest of the class.

All libraries contain books and different libraries contain different kinds of books. Some libraries also contain newspapers, magazines, periodicals, records, computer games, audio-tapes, video-tapes, paintings, games, local information – the list is endless.

> **2** Over the next two weeks, find out as much as you can about the services offered by all the libraries available to you.

You can go to the libraries in school and find out about them by:

- asking the librarian or teacher in charge;
- collecting any information sheets available.

The best way to find out about your local public library and the central public library is to visit them.

- Find out what you need to do to join the library.
- Ask if there are information sheets or booklets that tell you when it's open and what services it offers.

> **3** When you have got as much information as you can, write and design a **leaflet** that will encourage and help other people of your age to use the libraries in your school and community.

2 Practical information

Once you have found the information you want, can you always make sense of it?

> 1 In pairs or small groups, look at the five pieces of information below and over the page. For each one, write down one question than can be answered by using the information provided.

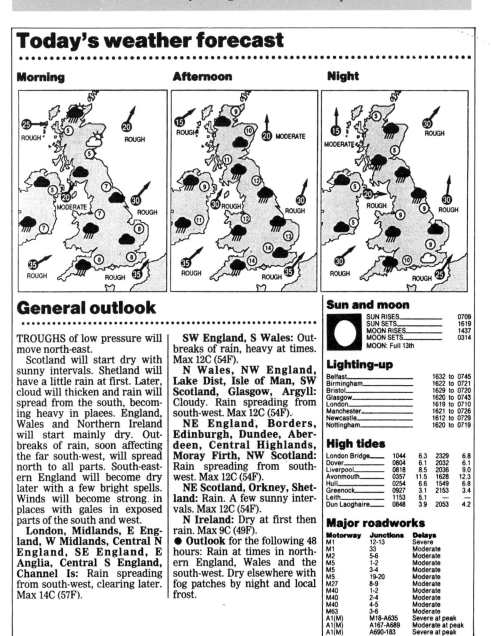

Today's weather forecast

Morning   **Afternoon**   **Night**

General outlook

TROUGHS of low pressure will move north-east.

Scotland will start dry with sunny intervals. Shetland will have a little rain at first. Later, cloud will thicken and rain will spread from the south, becoming heavy in places. England, Wales and Northern Ireland will start mainly dry. Outbreaks of rain, soon affecting the far south-west, will spread north to all parts. South-eastern England will become dry later with a few bright spells. Winds will become strong. in places with gales in exposed parts of the south and west.

London, Midlands, E England, W Midlands, Central N England, SE England, E Anglia, Central S England, Channel Is: Rain spreading from south-west, clearing later. Max 14C (57F).

SW England, S Wales: Outbreaks of rain, heavy at times. Max 12C (54F).

N Wales, NW England, Lake Dist, Isle of Man, SW Scotland, Glasgow, Argyll: Cloudy. Rain spreading from south-west. Max 12C (54F).

NE England, Borders, Edinburgh, Dundee, Aberdeen, Central Highlands, Moray Firth, NW Scotland: Rain spreading from south-west. Max 12C (54F).

NE Scotland, Orkney, Shetland: Rain. A few sunny intervals. Max 12C (54F).

N Ireland: Dry at first then rain. Max 9C (49F).

● **Outlook** for the following 48 hours: Rain at times in northern England, Wales and the south-west. Dry elsewhere with fog patches by night and local frost.

Sun and moon

SUN RISES	0709
SUN SETS	1619
MOON RISES	1437
MOON SETS	0314

MOON: Full 13th

Lighting-up

Belfast	1632 to 0745
Birmingham	1622 to 0721
Bristol	1629 to 0720
Glasgow	1620 to 0743
London	1619 to 0710
Manchester	1621 to 0726
Newcastle	1612 to 0729
Nottingham	1620 to 0719

High tides

London Bridge	1044	6.3	2329	6.8
Dover	0804	6.1	2032	6.1
Liverpool	0818	8.5	2036	9.0
Avonmouth	0357	11.5	1628	12.3
Hull	0254	6.6	1549	6.8
Greenock	0927	3.1	2153	3.4
Leith	1153	5.1	—	—
Dun Laoghaire	0848	3.9	2053	4.2

Major roadworks

Motorway	Junctions	Delays
M1	12-13	Severe
M1	33	Moderate
M2	5-6	Moderate
M5	1-2	Moderate
M5	3-4	Moderate
M5	19-20	Moderate
M27	8-9	Moderate
M40	1-2	Moderate
M40	2-4	Moderate
M40	4-5	Moderate
M63	3-6	Moderate
A1(M)	M18-A635	Severe at peak
A1(M)	A167-A689	Moderate at peak
A1(M)	A690-183	Severe at peak

For example:

Question: Tomorrow I am starting a two-day hiking holiday in Wales. What will the weather be like?

Answer: During the next 48 hours, there will be rain at times.

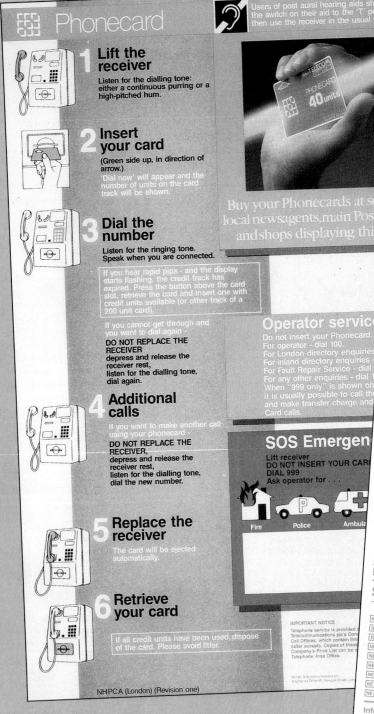

Phonecard

Users of post aural hearing aids should move the switch on their aid to the 'T' position and then use the receiver in the usual way.

1 Lift the receiver

Listen for the dialling tone: either a continuous purring or a high-pitched hum.

2 Insert your card

(Green side up, in direction of arrow.)

'Dial now' will appear and the number of units on the card track will be shown.

3 Dial the number

Listen for the ringing tone. Speak when you are connected.

If you hear rapid pips - and the display starts flashing, the credit track has expired. Press the button above the card slot, retrieve the card and insert one with credit units available (or other track of a 200 unit card).

If you cannot get through and you want to dial again -

DO NOT REPLACE THE RECEIVER depress and release the receiver rest, listen for the dialling tone, dial again.

4 Additional calls

If you want to make another call using your phonecard -

DO NOT REPLACE THE RECEIVER, depress and release the receiver rest, listen for the dialling tone, dial the new number.

5 Replace the receiver

The card will be ejected automatically.

6 Retrieve your card

If all credit units have been used, dispose of the card. Please avoid litter.

NHPCA (London) (Revision one)

PHONECARD 40 units

Buy your Phonecards at sele... local newsagents, main Post O... and shops displaying this s...

Operator service

Do not insert your Phonecard.
For operator - dial 100.
For London directory enquiries -
For inland directory enquiries -
For Fault Repair Service - dial
For any other enquiries - dial 1
When "999 only" is shown on
it is usually possible to call th...
and make transfer charge and
Card calls.

SOS Emergen...

Lift receiver
DO NOT INSERT YOUR CARI...
DIAL 999
Ask operator for . . .

Fire   Police   Ambula...

IMPORTANT NOTICE

Telephone service is provided
Telecommunications plc's Con...
Call Offices, which contain lim...
caller accepts. Copies of these...
Company's Price List can be o...
Telephone Area Office.

British Telecommunications plc
Registered Office 81 Newgate Street...

Oxford London

Thames Lines

Train services from 2 October 1989 to 13 May 1990

Mondays to Fridays

		Oxford depart	Paddington arrive
NE		0530D	0635
	BHX	0600	0707
	BHX	0610D	0729
	BHX	0635D	0744
NE		0640	0751
NE		0720	0817
IC		0738	0842
IC		0754	0852
		0831R	0940
NE		0854	0944
NE		0920	1014
IC		1000	1100
		1100	1200
		1200	1304
IC		1300	1359
IC		1400	1459
NE		1431	1530
IC		1500	1559
NE		1506	1603
IC		1600	1705
IC		1700	1800
IC		1745	1849
NE		1826	1939
NE		1915	2021
IC		2000	2100
		2026	2136
NE		2135	2235
IC		2233	2338

Saturdays

		Oxford depart	Paddington arrive
NE		0518D	0635
NE		0725	0827
IC		0754	0854
NE		0854	0950
NE		0915	1014
NE		1000	1100
NE		1100	1200
NE		1200	1304
NE		1300	1359
NE		1400	1459

Saturdays (cont'd)

		Oxford depart	Paddington arrive
IC		1431	1530
IC		1506	1603
NE		1600	1705
NE		1700	1805
IC		1800	1904
IC		1826	1939
NE		1900	1959
IC		2000	2100
		2028	2137
		2133D	2243
IC		2233	2343

Sundays

		Oxford depart	Paddington arrive
	G	0740D	0905
	K	0740D	0905
NE	K	0930	1051
NE	G	0955	1116
		1108R	1231
NE		1130	1246
NE		1250	1406
	N	1320R	1450
	Q	1320R	1500
NE		1430	1546
	J	1445R	1616
NE		1515D	1645
IC		1630	1738
NE		1706	1815
		1730	1830
		1740R	1855
IC		1817	1919
IC		1832	1930
NE		1912R	2017
IC		1950	2050
		1953R	2106
IC		2022	2124
IC		2027	2131
NE		2115	2219
IC		2138	2237
IC		2227	2333

Information

NE	Network Express.
IC	InterCity train; also conveys First Class accommodation. Seat reservations available. Snacks, sandwiches and hot and cold drinks available.
	Trolley service of cold snacks and hot and cold drinks available for whole or part of journey.
	Bus service (heavy luggage, prams, bicycles, etc. may not be conveyed).
BHX	Does not run on Bank Holiday Mondays 16 April and 7 May.

All services convey First Class accommodation.

OCTOBER 1989

PRICES FOR SPECIAL SERVICES

I REGISTERED POST

For posting important documents or valuables: from £1.55 (for items valued at up to £850) to £1.85 (for items valued at up to £2,250)
Consequential loss insurance (for those items that have a value higher than the material worth): from 45p (for £1,000 of cover), to £1.35 (for £10,000 of cover), plus first class postage and registration fees.

2 RECORDED DELIVERY

For signature on delivery: standard postage rate + 25p

3 ROYAL MAIL SPECIAL DELIVERY

For next day delivery: 1st class postage rate + £1.75

4 INTERNATIONAL SERVICES

Swiftair (Express Airmail):   standard Airmail rate + £1.75

Aerogrammes (stationery and envelope all-in-one)   30p each (£1.65 for a pack of 6)

Airmail	(Europe EEC)	20p	(20g)	
	(Europe non-EEC)	24p	(20g)	
		Letters 10g	Each extra 10g	
Rest of World:		32p	14p	
North Africa, Middle East		34p	16p	
Americas, Africa, India, SE Asia		37p	18p	
Australasia, Japan, China				
Surface mail	(letters outside Europe)	24p	(20g)	
	(worldwide postcard rate)	29p		

5 INLAND LETTERS

(UK, Channel Islands and Isle of Man)

	60g	100g	150g	200g
First class	20p	30p	37p	45p
Second class	15p	24p	28p	34p

Royal Mail Stamps
Have you remembered to buy some?

STAMPS ARE NOW AVAILABLE FROM ALL SHOPS DISPLAYING THIS SIGN

A

(Please note: all rates are correct at the time of going to press: 2/10/89. Your Post Office would be pleased to provide more details about all Royal Mail services.)

999

EMERGENCY SERVICES

Fire

Police

Ambulance

Cave Rescue

Coastguard
(sea and cliff rescue)

Mountain Rescue

Dial 999 or the emergency number shown on the number label

Tell the operator which service you want

Give the telephone number shown on the phone

Wait for the emergency service to answer

Give the address where help is needed

Give any other necessary information

Dialling 999 is free

To dial in darkness or in smoke, it will help if you know where the hole or button is on your phone. Remembering where it is and practising finding it with your eyes closed could make an enormous difference in a real emergency.

Other Emergency Services

For other emergencies, eg

Gas ■ Water ■ Electricity

see section 4   NAMES AND NUMBERS

Samaritans

Oxford **722122**   ■   Banbury **270000**

ChildLine

For children in trouble or danger – Speak to someone who cares
Phone us free on – **0800 1111**
or write to us free at – **ChildLine, Freepost 1111 London EC4B 4BB**

---

2 Swop your questions (not the answers) with another pair or group. Work out answers to each of the questions you've been set. Get together with the other pair or group, and go through the questions you set each other and the answers you came up with.

3 Over the next few days, collect at least three examples of different kinds of practical information – timetables, food wrappers and labels, holiday brochures, instruction booklets, the highway code – anything that gives people practical information. Make a class display of the examples collected, showing how practical information can be found everywhere and comes in all shapes and sizes.

How to follow instructions

Here are some instructions. Follow them carefully.

Draw a large circle. Draw two small circles. Inside each of the smaller circles, put a dot. The two small circles should be inside the larger circle, in the top third of the latter and slightly in from the outside. Ensure that the two circles are aligned. Draw another small circle – smaller than the two small ones – in the middle of the other ones, but slightly lower down. Underneath this circle (that's the third one, or fourth one if you include the large circle), draw a smallish rectangle.

Compare what you have each drawn. You've all followed the same instructions. Did you draw the same thing?

Discuss the instructions you were given. Use these questions to help you:

- Were there any words you didn't understand?
- Were the instructions in the right order?
- Were any of the instructions vague?
- Were any of the instructions irrelevant – could anything have been left out?

Instructions tell you what to do. They must be clear so that anyone can follow them and carry out the task correctly and easily. (To find out what you were meant to draw, look at page 83.)

Look at the five sets of different kinds of instructions on page 75. Notice that:

- symbols, diagrams, drawings and numbers, as well as words, are used to get meaning across.
- the way the instructions are set out – the **layout** – can help to make it easier to follow them.

Are the instructions on page 75 clear? Do you understand them?

1 Over the next few days, look out for two examples of instructions that you think are clear and easy to follow, and one example of instructions that you find difficult to understand. If possible, bring the examples to school. Otherwise, make a note of where you found them, what they're about and how they're set out.

2 Write a new, improved version of any instructions you have come across that you find difficult to follow. Think about **layout**, use of **diagrams**, **symbols**, and **illustrations**. Remember that the instructions must be clear so that other people can understand and follow them. Make them humorous if you think it will help others to make sense of them.

Filling out your Postal Order.

Once you have purchased a Postal Order:

1. Enter the name of the payee (the person/company to whom you are sending the Order) on both the Postal Order (A) and the counterfoil (B).

2. You may enter the name of the Post Office or town where the Order is to be cashed (C) if you are sending the Order to some one without a bank account.

3. Enter your name and address on the space provided on the reverse of the Postal Order (D).

IMPORTANT:
FILL OUT BOTH SIDES

What does 'crossing' a Postal Order mean?

If you're sending a Postal Order to someone with a bank account, an additional safeguard is to 'cross' the Postal Order. This is simply done by drawing two parallel lines vertically across the Order, and means that it cannot be cashed at a Post Office, but must be paid into a bank account. (This facility is particularly useful if you're sending money to a business, e.g. mail order companies.)

What if you make a mistake?

If you make a mistake, DO NOT try to rub it out or alter it, because payment may be refused. Take your Postal Order and counterfoil back to your Post Office and ask for a replacement Order to be issued.

What is the Counterfoil for?

Once you have completed your Postal Order, separate the counterfoil and send the Order only. Your counterfoil is your proof of purchase and should be kept in a safe place, as the serial number and date of issue will be required should you need to make any enquiries.

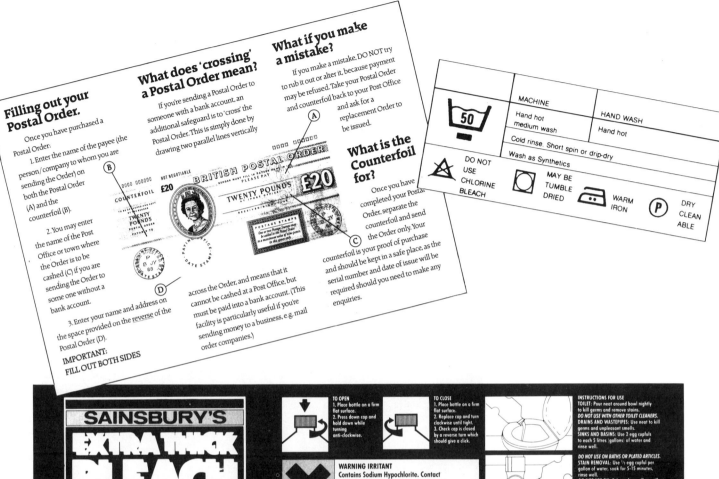

	MACHINE		HAND WASH
50	Hand hot medium wash		Hand hot
	Cold rinse. Short spin or drip-dry		
	Wash as Synthetics		

DO NOT USE CHLORINE BLEACH — MAY BE TUMBLE DRIED — WARM IRON — (P) DRY CLEAN ABLE

SAINSBURY'S EXTRA THICK BLEACH

INTENSIFIED TO KILL ALL GERMS EVEN AFTER THE FLUSH

1250 ml

NOT FOR INTERNAL CONSUMPTION

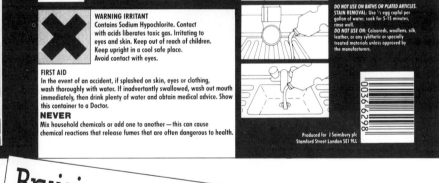

TO OPEN
1. Place bottle on a firm flat surface.
2. Press down cap and hold down while turning anti-clockwise.

TO CLOSE
1. Place bottle on a firm flat surface.
2. Replace cap and turn clockwise until tight.
3. Check cap is closed by a reverse turn which should give a click.

WARNING IRRITANT
Contains Sodium Hypochlorite. Contact with acids liberates toxic gas. Irritating to eyes and skin. Keep out of reach of children. Keep upright in a cool safe place. Avoid contact with eyes.

FIRST AID
In the event of an accident, if splashed on skin, eyes or clothing, wash thoroughly with water. If inadvertently swallowed, wash out mouth immediately, then drink plenty of water and obtain medical advice. Show this container to a Doctor.

NEVER
Mix household chemicals or add one to another — this can cause chemical reactions that release fumes that are often dangerous to health.

INSTRUCTIONS FOR USE
TOILET: Pour neat around bowl nightly to kill germs and remove stains.
DO NOT USE WITH OTHER TOILET CLEANERS.
DRAINS AND WASTEPIPES: Use neat to kill germs and unpleasant smells.
SINKS AND BASINS: Use 2 egg cupfuls to each 5 litres (gallons) of water and rinse well.
DO NOT USE ON BATHS OR PLATED ARTICLES.
STAIN REMOVAL: Use ½ egg cupful per gallon of water, soak for 5-15 minutes, rinse well.
DO NOT USE ON: Coloureds, woollens, silk, leather, or any synthetic or specially treated materials unless approved by the manufacturers.

Produced for J Sainsbury plc
Stamford Street London SE1 9LL

0036 6298

Bruising

This is bleeding just under the skin; or deeper, in the tissues following injury which does not break the skin. The area will often become blue/black after quite a short time.

ACTION
1 Place a cold compress on injury to minimise swelling.

2 Support the injured part in the most comfortable position for the casualty, in a sling if appropriate.

COLD COMPRESSES
These are placed on bruises or sprains to cool the area. This will minimise swelling and reduce the pain. Leave a compress on an injury

for about 30 minutes. If possible leave it uncovered, but if you need to secure it use an openweave material such as gauze bandage.

COLD WATER PACK
Soak a face cloth, thin towel or similar material in cold water, wring out until it stops dripping. Place it over injury. Replace pack every 10

IMPORTANT
A "black eye" is a bruise normally caused by a blow to the face but as it may also involve damage to the eye or skull, you should always make sure it is seen by a doctor.

minutes; or cool by dripping cold water on to it as necessary.

ICE PACKS
If you have any ice available you can make a very effective compress by filling a plastic bag half full of ice. Add a little salt — this makes ice melt faster — squeeze air out of bag and seal. Wrap bag in a towel. Place over injury.

COOKING INSTRUCTIONS:
Cook from frozen

Oven Method.
Spread chips evenly on baking sheet and bake in a pre-heated oven at 230°C, 450°F, Gas Mark 8 for 15-20 minutes until crisp and golden. For best results turn chips once during cooking.

Grill Method.
Remove grill mesh and spread chips evenly over bottom of tray. Cook under a hot grill for 8-12 minutes until crisp and golden, turning once during cooking.

How to explain things clearly

It's usually much easier to help someone to understand how to do something if you can *show* them how to do it, and can let them try doing it for themselves. If your science teacher wants to explain how to carry out an experiment, she or he will probably demonstrate how it's done so that you can see what happens as well as listen to the explanation. Sometimes, however, you have to rely entirely on the words you use and the way you use them.

1 From all the practical things you know how to do, pick one to explain to someone else. It could be anything, like how to:

- mend a puncture
- cook an omelette
- play 'monopoly'
- use a microscope
- open a bank account
- use a word processor
- set a video timer
- use a pay phone
- join the public library

Working in pairs, take it in turns to explain how to . . . (whatever you have decided above).

Next, discuss how clear you thought the explanations were and whether you could understand them.

When you're explaining things, you have to think about:

- the subject or **topic** you're explaining. What are the key points? What order should they be in?
- the people or **audience** who are listening to you. What do they already know? What needs to be explained to them? What sorts of questions are they most likely to want answers to?

2 Role play: It is 'community week' at your school. Two of you have been asked to explain what leisure facilities there are for young people in your area to:

■ a group of local business people.
■ a group of students of your age from another part of Britain.

Act out the two situations.

See Skills Session 11, Is it clear?, page 174.

Producing a brochure

Schools offer a lot of written information to parents. As well as the general school brochure, your school probably has information sheets or booklets about uniform, different school subjects, clubs and societies, school trips, guidelines for behaviour and so on.

All this information is usually put together by the teachers and headteacher. Here is your opportunity to write a brochure from your point of view.

1 Choose one of your school subjects to write about. Some of the questions you might think about to help you to decide what to include in your brochure are:

■ What kinds of things do you learn? What is the subject about?
■ How many lessons do you have each week?
■ What different kinds of work do you do?
■ What is the classroom (or laboratory or workshop) like?
■ What equipment do you need to take to lessons?
■ How can you get the best out of this subject?

2 Decide who this brochure is for, and what its purpose is. It could be either an impressive picture of the school subject for outsiders such as parents trying to decide whether they want to send their children to the school; or a helpful guide for pupils who are about to come to the school.

3 Think about the design and layout of your brochure. Are you going to include any photographs, diagrams or illustrations?

Produce a brochure of two to four sides. Remember that you want your chosen audience to read the brochure and to find the information useful. So, make it attractive to look at, interesting to read, and easy to understand.

3 Reading for different purposes

Do you always read in the same way? Do you, for example, read a telephone directory in the same way as you read a story? (If you do, you probably won't have time to make the phone call.)

When you're reading for information, you need to think about *why* you're reading – what your purpose is – before you begin. Then you'll have a better idea of *how* to read and *make sense of* the information in front of you.

Search reading

Most information books have an **index** at the back. An index is a list of the important subjects or topics in a book. It tells you where to find each subject.

> 1   Look at the index on page 79, which is from a book about computers. Write down the page numbers where you can read about *word processors*.

Think about *how* you read the index to find what you wanted.

You probably found what you wanted very quickly because you ran your eye down the page looking for *word processors* and did not pay attention to anything else on the page.

This kind of reading is called **search reading** or **scanning**. You search read a piece of writing when you want to find a particular piece of information, or answer to a particular question. You run your eye down the page with one question in mind, and pay no attention to anything else.

> 2   Search read the index again, and write down the page numbers where you can read about each of the following subjects:
>
> ■ cable television
> ■ games
> ■ teletext
> ■ robots

See Skills Session 9, How to use a dictionary, on page 170.

INDEX

Skim reading

Imagine that you're looking for information about the *solar system*.

- You find an encyclopaedia.
- You search read the index.
- You turn to the section on the solar system and come across the information printed on the opposite page.
- What do you do next?

You could read the whole section very carefully, making notes as you go along. But if you do, you'll probably find that you won't have a good understanding of what you read and your notes will be copied word for word from the book.

Instead, you can first read the whole section *quickly* to get a general idea of what it is about. This first quick reading is called **skim reading**.

Skim reading can help you to find out quickly what's in a piece of factual information so that:

- You get an overall idea of what it's about.
- You can decide whether it contains the information you need.
- You can spot what the important points are, and what you need to go back over to read carefully and slowly.

1   Look at the extract about the solar system on page 81. It is from the *World Book* encyclopaedia. Notice that:

- The writing is divided up into sections with headings and sub-headings.
- The writing is arranged in paragraphs.
- Words that the writer wants to emphasise are in *italics*.

These are all *clues* to help you to discover what the writing is about. They help you to pick out the *key* ideas.

2   Skim read the extract to get an overall understanding of what it is about. As you read:

- Keep asking questions (in your head) – What's this paragraph about? How does it link up with the others?
- Use the clues that are there to help you go through the reading – headings, sub-headings, paragraphs, words in italics.

In pairs or small groups, take it in turns to tell each other what you think are the key points made by the writer, and which sections you would need to go back to for a more careful reading before making notes.

THE SOLAR SYSTEM

Solar system is the sun and all the objects that travel around it. The solar system includes (1) the earth and eight other *planets*, along with the *satellites* (moons) that travel around most of them; (2) planet-like objects called *asteroids*; (3) chunks of iron and stone called *meteoroids*; (4) bodies of dust and frozen gases called *comets*; and (5) drifting particles called *interplanetary dust*, and a drifting gas called *interplanetary plasma*.

The solar system has a circular shape. It is only a tiny part of a *galaxy* (family of stars) called the *Milky Way*. The Milky Way consists of more than 100 billion stars that are somewhat similar to the sun. The Milky Way, which also has a circular shape, is about 100,000 light-years across, and about 16,000 light-years thick as its center. A *light-year* is the distance light travels in one year at a speed of 186,282 miles (299,792 kilometers) per second. The solar system is less than one *light-day* (the distance light travels in one day) across. It is about 30,000 light-years from the center of the Milky Way. The galaxy turns, and the solar system travels around the center of the Milky Way about every 250 million years.

Many stars in the Milky Way are the centers of solar systems. Some astronomers think many of these systems may have some form of life. The nearest solar system that might have intelligent life is about 100 light-years away. It would take 100 years for a radio message sent from the earth at the speed of light to reach this solar system, and another 100 years for a reply to reach the earth.

Parts of the solar system

The sun is the center of the solar system. Its *mass* is more than 750 times as great as that of all the planets combined (see **Mass**). The huge mass of the sun creates the gravitation that keeps the other objects traveling around the sun in an orderly manner.

The sun continuously gives off energy in several forms – visible light; invisible *infrared*, *ultraviolet*, *X* and *gamma* rays; radio waves; and plasma (not electrically charged gas). The flow of plasma which becomes planetary plasma and drifts throughout the solar system, is called the *solar wind* (see **Solar wind**).

The surface of the sun changes continuously. Bright spots called *plages* and dark spots called *sunspots*, frequently form and disappear. Gases often shoot up violently from the surface. For a complete description of the sun, see the article **Sun**.

Planets are the second largest objects in the solar system. The four planets nearest the sun – Mercury,

Venus, Earth, and Mars – are the smallest planets, although Pluto's size has not been accurately determined. Those four planets are called *terrestrial* (earthlike) planets, and appear to consist chiefly of iron and rock. The earth has one satellite, and Mars has two. Mercury and Venus have no satellites.

The four largest planets – Jupiter, Saturn, Uranus, and Neptune – are called the *major* planets. They are probably made up chiefly of hydrogen, helium, ammonia, and methane. Compared to the terrestrial planets, they contain little iron and rock. Each of the major planets has several satellites. Pluto, the farthest planet from the sun, appears to be somewhat like the terrestrial planets. But because Pluto is so far away, astronomers know little about it and do not include it in either group.

All the planets except Pluto are surrounded by varying kinds and amounts of gases. The earth is the only planet that has enough oxygen surrounding it and enough water on its surface to support life as we know it. For a more complete description of the planets, see **Planet** and the separate articles on each planet.

Asteroids, also called *planetoids*, are small, irregularly shaped objects. Most asteroids are between the orbits of Mars and Jupiter. Astronomers have figured out the orbits of about 2,700 asteroids. About 30 asteroids have diameters greater than 120 miles (190 kilometers). Many others are less than 1 mile (1.6 kilometers) across. The asteroid belt between Mars and Jupiter also includes rings of dust. Astronomers believe the rings were formed by continuing collisions between asteroids, or by a single collision between two asteroids or between an asteroid and a comet.

Meteoroids are small chunks of iron and rock thought to result from collisions between asteroids. They also may be formed when comets disintegrate into fragments. Many meteoroids fall into the earth's atmosphere, but most are burned up by friction before they reach the earth. Meteoroids are called *meteors* while falling through the atmosphere, and *meteorites* if they are found on the earth's surface. See **Meteor**.

Comets. Most comets have three parts: (1) a solid *nucleus*, or center; (2) a round *coma*, or head, that surrounds the nucleus and consists of dust particles mixed with frozen water, frozen methane, and frozen ammonia; and (3) a long *tail* of dust and gases that escape from the head. Most comets stay near the outside of the solar system. Some come near the sun, where their bright heads and long, shining tails provide a rare and spectacular slight. See **Comet**.

4 Selecting the books you need

In pairs, one of you be the *searcher*, the other the *recorder*.

Searcher: find three books in the library that contain information that you need.

Recorder: make notes on what the searcher does.

If there is time, do this twice. Swap roles the second time so that you have the chance to be both searcher and recorder.

Notes for the searcher

1   Decide on your own topic for research, or choose one from the list below:
    ■ gorillas
    ■ nuclear energy
    ■ ancient Egypt
    ■ the Stock Exchange
    ■ the Globe Theatre in Shakespeare's time
    ■ Dorothy Hodgkinson's achievements as a scientist

2   Find three books that contain information about the topic you have chosen.

3   Make a note of the titles of the three books you choose.

4   Write down the page numbers in the books that contain the information you want.

Notes for the recorder

1   Watch the searcher very carefully.

2   Make a note of everything he or she does when searching for information. Include whether the searcher:
    ■ uses the library catalogue system;
    ■ rejects some books before selecting three;
    ■ uses the index and contents section of the books.

3   Record when your partner looks puzzled or fed up.

4   Time how long it takes the searcher to find the information she or he is looking for. (Start timing from the moment you enter the library.)

Afterwards, in your pairs:

1   Discuss what happened, using the notes made by the recorder.

2   Discuss and decide on the most efficient way of tracking down information in the library.

3   Jot down three to five points that would help someone who was searching for information in the library.

4   Report back to the rest of the class, going through the points you have written down.

5 How to make notes

Selecting and rejecting

The telephone rings. You answer it. This is what the person on the other end of the line says:

I'm in a 'phone box and I'm running out of change – I'm always short of change, aren't you? Anyway, I can't spend ages chattering. I'm ringing up to ask you if – I'm ever so sorry if I've dragged you away from the television – where was I? – oh yes – if you could give a message to Mrs White next door. I'm her daughter, you see, and we live in Barnstaple, and she hasn't got a 'phone, and your Mum said I could leave a message for my mother if ever I needed to. You see – that's really kind of your mum – I do appreciate it. I keep telling my mother she ought to get a 'phone, but she doesn't want one – s'ppose that's up to her, and we haven't got one after all. Well, as I was saying, we're supposed to be coming up tomorrow to see Mum. Coming up for the day we were, and really looking forward to it. Mum always puts on a lovely tea for us – cakes, trifles, sandwiches – all the things I loved when I was at home before I got married. As I said, we were coming up to see her tomorrow, but the cat's ill. I don't know what to do – I've called the vet twice, but not a sign of him – don't know what they do with their time. I haven't slept a wink all night, worrying about the cat and going round mopping up her mess – she keeps being sick, you see – all over the new fitted carpet – we've only had it a couple of months. She can't help it though and she looks so sad, poor love – she doesn't understand, you see. (Pause) The money's going – I haven't got anymore change. Make sure my mother gets the message, won't you? Bye.

Alongside the telephone is a note-pad and pen for writing down messages. What's the most important thing to tell Mrs White? Write a brief note of the message to give to her.
In pairs, compare the messages you've written down.

Making notes means making decisions. You have to decide what to *select* and what to *reject*.

Making sense of what you hear

Situation: A visitor comes to the school to give a talk on 'Word Games'. You have been told to make notes of the talk.

Choose one of the class (or the teacher) to be the person giving the talk. Everyone else makes notes of what she or he says.

GUIDELINES FOR THE NOTE-MAKERS

1 Concentrate and listen for key points.

2 Write down the most important points made by the speaker.

3 Make sure that you have understood a point before you write it down.

4 Make sure this book is closed while the talk is going on.

GUIDELINES FOR THE SPEAKER

1 Take time to read it through before you begin your talk. (Suggestions about when to pause or when to write up words on the blackboard are printed in *italics* and enclosed in brackets.)

2 Make sure everyone else has closed this book before you begin.

3 Read it to the class as if you were an outside speaker giving a talk.

4 When you have finished the talk, tell the class to open their books again.

'Word Games'– the text of the talk

Good morning, everyone. Is there anyone here who likes jokes? (*pause*) Well, I'm not going to be telling you any – mainly because I'm sure you're better at it than I am, but if you like jokes it means that you enjoy playing with language. That's what jokes are, one of the ways we mess about with or play with language. Today, I'm going to be talking about another way in which we play with the English language – word games.

Word games are amazingly popular with people of all ages. Many of the game shows on television are based on language – 'Blankety Blank', 'Call My Bluff', 'Lucky Ladders' and 'Catch Phrase' are all word games. Pick up a newspaper or magazine and you're sure to come across a word puzzle or competition. I expect that some of you play word games at home with your family now and again, and I'm sure you've all played games like 'hangman' on the last day of term at school. There are hundreds of different kinds of word games – today we're just going to look at six of them.

Let's begin with the most popular of all word games, 'crosswords'. The first crossword appeared in an American newspaper in 1913, and was devised by a journalist called Arthur Wynne. From the beginning, crosswords, or 'wordcrosses' as they were called at first, were very popular. The people who think up the clues for crosswords obviously have to know a lot about words, but they also need to be very imaginative and inventive. The clues have to be very clever and puzzling, but they mustn't mislead the readers, and getting that balance right isn't easy.

'Words within words' (*write up on the board*) is another very popular word game. Here you are given a single word and you simply have to see how many words you can make from the letters of the word given to you. Let's take the word 'happiness', for example. (*Write happiness on the board*) You set about making words from it like 'nap', 'sap' and so on. (*Write nap and sap on the board. Pause to give the class chance to take them in.*)

There are a number of games that are 'grid games'. All grid games are based on the principle of building up words on a grid. You can play some grid games on your own, games like word search when you have to find words hidden in a grid of letters by moving from one square to the next in any direction – up, down, sideways, diagonally, backwards or forwards. Other grid games are for people to play against each other – games such as Boggle, Kan-U-Go and Lexicon. The most famous of all grid games is Scrabble. This game is so popular that there are national and international scrabble competitions – the words and scores that the best players come up with are mind-boggling.

With 'anagrams,' you have to re-arrange the letters of a word or phrase to make new words. The best anagrams are those which are linked in meaning to the original word or words that you are given. So an anagram for astronomers could be moon-starers. (*Write astronomers and moon-starers on the board*) Here you can see how all the letters in astronomers have been moved around to produce moon-starers (*pause*).

When words or phrases read the same in both directions, they are 'palindromes' (*write palindrome on the board*). For example, Mum is the same backwards and forwards, as is Dad (*write Mum, Dad on the board*). So, the words mum and dad are palindromes. It gets a bit more difficult when you start trying to find palindromes with more than three letters – madam is one (*write madam on the board*) – and it gets really difficult when you try to go beyond a single word and think up whole sentences that can be read the same in both directions. Have a look at this sentence on the board (*write Draw, O coward! on the board*). Can you see that it is a palindrome? (*pause*) It's said that the longest palindrome in the English language contains more than 65,000 words, but I find that difficult to believe.

The final word game I want to mention is 'doublets' (*write doublets on the board*). In doublets one word is changed into another word in a series of steps, each word different from the previous one by a single letter. So to play doublets you have to form a chain of linked words trying to keep the chain as small as possible. If this sounds complicated, have a look at this example thought up by the inventor of the game, Lewis Carroll, the author of the books about Alice.

(*Write on the board: Problem: Drive PIG into STY*
Solution: PIG-WIG-WAG-WAY-SAY-STY)

Again, this is a very simple game to set up, but it's not always easy to be good at it.

As I said at the beginning, we're always playing with words. Today I've simply looked at six different kinds of word games. I hope that you'll have a go at some of these games, and if you're feeling really inspired, maybe you'll try inventing some word games of your own. (*pause*) Thank you.

In pairs or small groups, discuss the notes you have made. If you disagree with each other about the most important points made by the speaker, try to explain the reasons for your selection of key points. (It may help to refer to the text of the talk when you are discussing your notes.)
Report back to the rest of the class. Tell them what your group has decided are the most important points made by the speaker in the talk.

You make notes to help you in your learning. They have to make sense to you so that you can use them.

Test out the usefulness of the notes you made of the talk on word games by using them to do the following exercise:

1   Write down three words that are *palindromes*.
2   *Doublets:* turn 'boy' into 'man'.
3   Write down your first name and surname. Try making an *anagram* of your names.
4   *Words within words:* make as many words as you can from 'language'.
5   *Word search:* write down all the languages you can find in this grid. There are fifteen languages hidden.

J	T	U	R	K	I	S	H	R	O
M	A	R	A	B	I	C	F	U	I
A	A	P	Z	Y	P	R	Q	S	T
B	M	L	A	O	E	L	F	S	A
E	S	P	A	N	I	S	H	I	L
N	G	H	C	Y	E	T	H	A	I
G	C	H	I	N	E	S	E	N	A
A	H	S	I	L	G	N	E	J	N
L	G	E	R	M	A	N	X	W	P
I	D	N	I	H	U	R	D	U	O

In pairs or in small groups, discuss the most important things you need to think about and do when making notes.
Produce an information sheet about making notes to put up on the classroom wall. You may decide to set out your advice as a list of do's and don'ts. For example:

Do   **Don't**
Make sure you understand before   Copy out chunks from books
you write notes

Design your sheet in any way you wish, as long as the advice is clear and can help others in your class to make useful notes.

6 The World of Books

You should now know quite a lot about tracking down and making sense of information. This is your chance to really use the information sheets you've produced and the skills you've tried out by investigating 'The World of Books'. When you've written up your final reports, you could make them into a class display for an Open Day or Parents' Evening.

Readers
Who reads books?
How much money do people spend on books?
Which books do people in your class enjoy reading?
Is reading less popular than it used to be?

Best-sellers
Which kind of books sell best?
Which books are in the top ten at the moment?
Do fashions change in the kind of books people read?
Which books have sold more copies than any other throughout the world in the last fifty years?

Publishing
What do publishers do?
What different kinds of jobs are there in the publishing industry?
How do publishers decide what to publish?

Writers
How do people become writers?
Do writers make a lot of money?

1 In pairs or small groups, discuss all the kinds of questions you could try to find answers to when carrying out an investigation into 'The World of Books'. This is called **brainstorming.** The topics and questions on this page will help you to get started.
Jot down four or five questions that you think are worth finding out about. Report back to the rest of the class.

2 Prepare an **action plan**.
- Decide what you want to concentrate on, from the list made by the class.
- Think about how you could get the information you're after (interview people? prepare a questionnaire? visit book shops or printers?). Be realistic about the available time.
- Write a draft action plan and discuss it with your teacher.
- Then write your action plan, including your area of investigation, method(s) of collecting information, and a list of all the things you need to do.

3 Write the **report**.
- When you have collected your information, you can begin to think about how to organise it for your report. Are you going to have headings, illustrations or photographs, a front cover, a contents list, a glossary of technical terms? Sketch out a plan of how you intend to arrange and present your research material.
- Write the first draft of your report.
- Go over the first draft, looking to see whether you have organised and presented the information in the best possible way. You might want to discuss this with someone.
- Produce your final report.
- Read through the final report and then write ten to fifteen lines about what you think of it.

If you need help writing the report,
go to Skills Session 10, Impersonal writing, on page 172.

Book shops
How many book shops are there in your area?
Are there any book shops especially for young people?
How many books do they sell each year?
How do they encourage people to buy books?

Libraries
Who decides which books a library stocks?
Who owns libraries?
What kind of books are borrowed most often?
How many people belong to a library?

pleasures and preferences

Contents

Introduction

The emphasis in this Project is on enjoyment.

In recent years there has been an explosion in the entertainment industry; today a vast range of books, magazines, films, videos, records, television and radio programmes are readily available for people to select and enjoy.

The purpose of this Project is to help you to reflect on your experience of the things you read, watch or listen to, and to think about the choices you make and the preferences you have.

Products

You will be trying out different ways of voicing your opinion about books, magazines, music, television, radio, films and video, and ways of sharing your enjoyment of these things with other people. You will be writing reviews, devising programmes and organising a day out. A lot of the material you produce can be added to the dossier compiled in *Focusing on experience*.

Audience

Most of the time you will be producing a range of material for other members of the class to think about and enjoy.

1 Home, sweet home

Read the article below, taken from *The Indy*, a weekly newspaper for young people.

Teenagers strangely happy with their lot

☐ **Sean O'Neill**

YOUNG PEOPLE today are strangely content. Unlike many generations before them, they don't seem to have many arguments with the way their lives are run.

The British teenagers' lot is a happy one, and parents are not the ogres we all love to think they are, according to the second exclusive *Indy* survey on the mood of our readership.

Indeed, home is such a sweet place that 79 per cent of you do not want to leave it before the age of 18. One person does not want to leave at all. Only three per cent say the atmosphere in their homes is unfriendly.

The Indy asked 500 12-15-year-olds how happy they were at home, and their parents came up smelling of roses. Ninety-two per cent of Indy teenagers are happy with the amount their parents listen to them. Seventy-two per cent feel they have enough status at home.

More than half of parents share interests with their kids, ranging from drag racing and physics, to art and flower arranging.

Rarely are parents considered to be too tough: 74 per cent of our teenagers say discipline at home is about right, and 13 per cent complain their parents aren't tough enough.

Parents are held in such high regard that 66 per cent of our teenagers would consider looking after them when they grow too old to live by themselves.

But while parents might take comfort from our findings, not everyone will be happy at what the survey reveals.

Teachers might not like to know that parents supervise homework in only 21 per cent of cases.

Feminists should be displeased to learn that teenagers generally consider their fathers to be boss of the house. In only 26 per cent of homes was power shared equally between both parents.

Authoritarians will be angry to discover that 47 per cent of our teenagers are not expected home until 10 pm or later.

I want you to interview an 11-15 year old as a follow-up to the 'Teenagers strangely happy with their lot' story.
1. The finished article needs to be 250-350 words long.
2. Remember it's a follow-up to the survey, so make sure you ask about the same kinds of things - how they get on with their parents, the rules in the house, discipline, what they do in their spare time etc.
Get on to it straight away!

The Editor

Imagine that you are a reporter working for a newspaper for young people. You receive the note on the left from the editor.

1   Prepare your questions for the **interview**:

■ First, read through the article again and make a note of the kinds of things asked about in the survey.
■ Second, jot down eight to twelve questions for your interview.
■ Third, go through your list of questions and decide which one you're going to ask first, which one next, and so on.

2   In pairs, interview each other.
You need to keep a record of the answers you get when you're doing the interviewing. Either, make notes of what your partner says or tape the interview and make a transcript of it afterwards.

3   Write up the interview.

■ You'll probably have far too much material for an article of 250–350 words. Go through your notes or transcript, and decide which bits to cut down or cut out.
■ Decide how you're going to set out your article, and how you want it to look on the page of the newspaper. You could present it as an interview.

See Skills Session 16, How to interview people, on page 181.

Here are two ways you could set out your article:

Home, sweet home

Sally West quizzes Winston Davey, aged 12, on the kind of life he leads at home.

Rules and discipline

My parents are pretty good and reasonable. I'm allowed out on Fridays and Saturdays until 9.30. During the week I usually stay in.

No complaints

This week's in-depth interview
Chris Barnes is 13 and goes to Woodbridge Comprehensive School in the Midlands. Mark Robinson interviewed her about the kind of life she leads at home. Chris has got some very interesting things to say, so read on . . .

Mark: What do you think of the rules in your house?

Chris: OK, because there aren't any really.

Mark: Are you allowed to go out when you want to?

Chris: More or less. I'm keen on judo and belong to a judo club. I go there twice a week. I've even persuaded my Mum to take up judo, so we go together.

If you prefer, you could set it out as a piece of continuous writing, as below.

What's your home life like?

☐ Stuart Prower

As a follow up to our survey on what teenagers think of the way their lives are run, I interviewed Jo Widdowson, a thirteen year old from London. Jo lives with her father and two brothers – aged 14 and 16 – and finds life pretty hectic at home. She describes her father as easy-going and always ready to listen to her, but her brothers get her down sometimes, especially when they expect her to do all the housework because she's a girl . . .

If it's possible to photocopy your finished article, give a copy to the person you interviewed so that they can include it in their *Focusing on experience* folder.

2 Personally speaking . . .

Changing taste

What kinds of clothes do you like wearing? What kinds of clothes did you like wearing three or four years ago? It's likely that your *taste* in clothes has changed over the years. As people change, the kinds of things they like tend to change as well.

1 Jot down the names of your favourite television programme. If you have two or three favourites, write them all down.

2 Think back to when you were younger, between seven and ten, and jot down the names of the television programmes that were your favourites then.

3 Now go through the list below, and for each item, write down your current favourite (or favourites) and then the names or titles of your favourites when you were younger:

■ music – particular singles, bands or singers;
■ comics and magazines;
■ films and videos;
■ radio programmes;
■ fiction – particular stories, poems, books or writers.

Prepare a radio or television programme called 'Changing Taste' to present to the class. In this 5–10 minute programme, people talk about the way their taste in music, television, books and so on has changed. In small groups, first discuss what you wrote down about your changing taste. Second, decide what you're going to include in your programme, and how you're going to present it.

The following questions may help you:

■ Is it a radio or television programme?
■ Are you going to present it directly to the class or put it on tape (audio or video)?
■ Are you going to talk about *all* the categories – music, comics and magazines, films and videos, radio programmes, television programmes, books – or are you going to concentrate on one or two of them?
■ Who is going to be the presenter of the programme? Is the presenter going to chair the discussion?
■ Who is going to talk about what?

Make your programme as interesting and as lively as possible and present it in a polished way. Use introductory music if you can.

Reviews

Newspapers and magazines are full of **reviews** of films, singles, albums, television and radio programmes, plays, performances and books. A review tells you what someone thinks about a new record, film and so on. The people who write reviews – critics or reviewers – are expressing their *personal opinions*.

Here is your opportunity to write some reviews – to say what you think – for the other members of your class. Read the reviews below and on page 94, taken from a number of magazines and newspapers.

video*clips*

★ DANNY, THE CHAMPION OF THE WORLD

Finally from Collins this month we find **DANNY, THE CHAMPION OF THE WORLD** (U). Adapted from a Roald Dahl story, this is a home-grown production that features ace performances from the likes of Robbie Coltrane, Jimmy Nail, Jean Marsh, Lionel Jeffries, Michael Hordern and (nepotism time!) Cyril Cusack, his son-in-law Jeremy Irons and *his* son Samuel—you can check out what Cyril's daughter (Jeremy's wife) looks like on the 'Stars Out' pages this month...

Described by some as 'the first quality British film for all the family since *The Railway Children*', Collins are also taking the unusual step of releasing it at a sell-through price as well.

Singles

Scoop ratings ☆☆☆☆☆ **Buy!**
☆☆☆☆ **Tape off the radio!** ☆☆☆
Turn radio up! ☆☆ **Turn radio off!** ☆
Throw radio at wall!

RAMONES: 'Pet Sematary' (Chrysalis) ☆☆☆

The Ramones are an American punk-ish band known for their fast and furious songs. *Pet Sematary* is quite a relaxed, low key song, and for a moment it seemed as though their thrash days were behind them. But then when you hear the other side, *All Screwed Up*, with its pounding drums and talk of suicide... you realise that things haven't changed too much! It's about time they learnt to spell, though – Cemetery starts with a C or it did when we were at school.

Last Night's View ...

BLACKADDER slithered back last night having shed another skin and donned the uniform of a First World War captain for Blackadder Goes Forth (BBC1). We find him in the trenches trenchantly opposed to risking his neck and surrounded as ever by buffoons.

It has clearly been harder to freshen the formula this time but with the old firm of Stephen Fry, Hugh Laurie, Tim McInnerny and Tony Robinson in support Rowan Atkinson looks set for another successful run. I would repeat a few lines but for the certainty that it is not so much the script, more the way that Atkinson delivers it that is funny.

FILMS

Daniel Rosenthal and Paula Rodney round up this week's releases

The Bear (PG)

Now THE most successful film of all time in France, Jean-Jacques Annaud's *The Bear* has a simple synopsis: two bears, two hunters, the forest, the bears' point of view.

The Bear has the most beautiful locations since Roland Joffe's *The Mission*; the Italian Dolomites providing a stunning backdrop against which Nature's brutality, beauty and integrity are displayed in equal measure.

With little dialogue, the film is heavily dependent on music to enhance its visual impact but, sadly, certain scenes are spoiled by Philippe Sarde's jarring music. That apart, *The Bear* is perhaps the most daring and imaginative "animal" movie ever made. Worth it.

LISA STANSFIELD: All Around The World (Arista)

Lisa Stansfield comes from "oop North". This is common knowledge. Yet at the beginning of this record Lisa starts speaking in an American accent. This seems rather silly. However, the single gets a little more sensible as it progresses. It's quite similar to her last hit "This Is The Right Time" in that it's a slower kind of dance "vibe" which is all rather pleasant, it's just such a shame that it makes you want to fall asleep.

Best boy in the world

DANNY THE Champion of the World is the title and that is certainly what Danny's father thinks Danny is by the end of the story.

At the beginning of the book, Danny tells you about his life when he was younger. His father is a mechanic and unfortunately his mother died when he was a baby.

Danny's life is an exciting one. He lives with his father in a little caravan (a bit like the old Gypsy one) next to a petrol station which his father owns.

Danny thinks that his life will be even more exciting when he's nine. But his father has a secret. A deep dark secret which leads them into a bit of trouble.

Danny's father's secret involved creeping up to Hazell's woods at twilight, to find secret

Alison Curry, 11, from Newcastle.

ways of catching pheasants like the 'horsehair stopper' the 'sticky hat' the 'sleeping beauty' and the great 'Opening Day Shooting Party.'

Read it for yourself and find out how Danny and his father get their revenge on Mr Victor Hazell!! The meanest man in the country!!

Danny The Champion Of The World by Roald Dahl and with marvellous illustrations by Jill Bennett, and is published by Puffin.

1   Choose a record that you've heard recently, or a book that you've read, or a television programme or film that you've seen that you think is really *boring*. Write a short, snappy review of it in no more than 80 words. Make clear to the readers – the other people in your class – what you think of it, why you found it so boring.

2   This time, choose a television programme or film that you think is worth watching, or a book that you would recommend to other people of your age. Give your readers an outline of the programme, film or book, and tell them why it is one not to be missed. Aim at writing 100–200 words. So that everyone can read the reviews, display them in the classroom or put them into a class review file that you can all add to during the school year. If you have a school magazine or newspaper, perhaps you can get your reviews published.

Are you sitting comfortably?

It's not only young children who enjoy having stories read to them. Television and radio programmes in which people read stories – programmes such as *Cat's Whiskers*, *Jackanory* and *A Book at Bedtime* – are very popular.

> You are going to create and present a 10–15 minute programme of stories you have written.

1 In small groups, decide who the programme is for. The audience could be:

- your class or another class in school;
- parents at a Parents' Evening or 'Open Day';
- older people in your community who have trouble with their sight and find difficulty in reading;
- a group of pupils in another school – perhaps in another country – that your school or class has links with.

2 Decide whether you're going to make a tape (audio or video) or present a live performance of the stories you have written.

3 Look through the stories you have written recently and, with your chosen audience in mind, select one or two that you think would work well when read aloud, and would make an interesting 10–15 minute programme. You could use one that you may have written for *Telling stories*.

4 Discuss how you're going to present your story-telling programme. You could consider:

- the use of music and sound effects;
- having an announcer to introduce and close the programme;
- using different people to read any dialogue in the story;
- dividing up the story so that you each read part of it.

5 Before you tape or present your programme, run through it once or twice to make sure that the final product is as polished as you can make it.

3 A great day out

A day to remember

Describe a day out that you've experienced that really stays in your memory as a great day: a family outing, a day out with friends, a school trip.

1 Bring the memory alive for your readers – the other members of your class – so that they can get a feel of the enjoyment you had on that day.

2 In pairs, read each other's descriptions to see whether the sense of enjoyment and pleasure comes across to the reader. Suggest any improvements you think could be made to the writing to make it more lively and interesting.

3 Write your final description (250–400 words), which you can add to the folder of your work that you produce when working through *Focusing on experience*.

The best ever school visit

> Imagine that your class is going to have a day out of school, planned and organised by you. You can arrange whatever you want to, as long as:
> - it doesn't cost more that £10 per head;
> - it's a day out that the class will thoroughly enjoy.

1 Decide where you're going to go, how you're going to get there, and what you're going to do. Be realistic about the length of the journey. You won't, for example, be able to go to Disneyland on a day trip. Write a programme or **itinerary** for the day. For example:

    8.00   Coaches leave school car park
    10.00 Arrive at Alton Towers

   (and so on for the whole day, ending with the time of arrival back at school.)

2 Write a letter to be sent to the parents/guardians of the pupils in your class informing them of the day out. In the letter include all the information that parents/guardians will need before being able to decide whether they want their daughter/son to go on this trip.

3 Prepare an information sheet for the pupils going on the trip. In it, include information about:

   - time and place of departure and return;
   - the things they need to take with them – equipment, packed lunch and so on;
   - what they're expected to wear – school uniform, mountain boots, anoraks . . .;
   - how you expect them to behave.

   Be as detailed and as clear as possible so that no one will turn up in unsuitable clothing or without all the things they might need.

4 Make a poster advertising your day out, and encouraging the members of your class to sign up for it.

5 Prepare a short talk to give to the class. Tell them what they'll be missing if they don't go, and persuade them that the day you're organising is better than all of the others.

4 Films, videos and censorship

Well worth seeing

1   Jot down the titles of any films you have seen – at the cinema or on video – over the past few months. From your list, select the one that you enjoyed most of all, and make a note of why you think it was a good film.

2   In pairs, discuss what you have written down. Ask each other about the films you have selected. You could ask:

- What kind of film was it – horror, war, western, romance, true-to-life, science fiction, musical, disaster, thriller, detective?
- Who were the main characters?
- What, briefly, was the story about?
- Who were the stars of the film? Were they good?
- Which particular parts of the film did you enjoy most?
- Did the film make you laugh, cry, or what?

On your own, write a short piece (100–200 words) about the film you selected and why you enjoyed it so much.

The perfect film

Mammoth Film Productions want to make a film that is going to be a sure-fire box office success with the eleven to fifteen age group. To make sure that they produce the kind of film that will be popular with this age group, they have hired you as consultants, to advise them on the kind of film to make.

1   In small groups, discuss the kind of films that you enjoy.

2   Mammoth Film Productions only have enough money to make one film, so now work out what kind of film is likely to be really popular. Decide on the stars, what kinds of characters they'll play, what will happen to them, and so on. Give the film a title.

3   Report back to the rest of the class. You can test out whether you've come up with the right idea for a successful film by seeing whether the other members of your class would be keen to see this film you've created.

4   After you've heard what everyone else in the class has to say – about their films and yours – you may decide to look again at your film and make a few changes. When you're satisfied that you've come up with a winner, it's time to publicise it.

Either each person design a poster in which you include the title of the film, the names of the stars and a brief summing up of the story, or as a group, write and act out a short television commercial for your film.

Not in front of the children

Look at the advertisements below for different films. Notice that each one has a symbol which tells you which age group the film is suitable for.

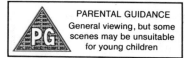

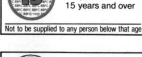

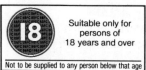

Members of a group called the British Board of Film Classification view every film and video before it is released in Britain and decide which of the certificates shown on the left should be given to it.

You are members of the Young People's Film and Video Committee. Your job is to make sure that six to eight year olds do not watch films that you consider are unsuitable for them.

1   In small groups, discuss whether you think any of the films and videos you have watched recently are unsuitable for six to eight year olds.

2   Then discuss the kinds of things that would make a film or video unsuitable viewing for this age group. The following statements may help you:

- The language of the film is too adult.
- The film would encourage children to behave badly.
- The film is about a subject that six to eight year olds are too young and inexperienced to understand.
- The film would frighten or worry children and give them nightmares.

3   Draw up a list of those ingredients that film producers making films for young children should, in your opinion, avoid including in their films. Where possible, give examples to help the film producers understand the points you are making.

4   Report back to the rest of the class.

There has been a General Election. The Strict Party coalition (if you haven't come across this party before, turn to page 139) has been defeated. The new party in power is the Freedom for Young People's Party. This newly-elected government has said that it intends scrapping the British Board of Film Classification, and that young people should be allowed to watch whatever films and videos they want to.

Write two letters that could be sent to a local newspaper.
For the first one, put yourself in the place of someone who welcomes the Government's proposal, and thinks it's a good idea to let people of your age watch whatever they want. Write the kind of letter you think they would write to a local newspaper.
For the second one, put yourself in the position of someone who is very concerned about the Government's decision to do away with the British Board of Film Classification. He or she believes that eleven to fifteen year olds are not able to decide for themselves what films and videos they should watch. Write the kind of letter you think they would write to a local newspaper.

If you are having trouble writing the letters turn to Skills Session 19, How to write formal letters , on page 184.

5 Mega-brill mags

Hitting the right note

There are hundreds of different magazines and periodicals on sale in this country, each one aimed at a particular group of the population. *Blue Jeans*, for example, is aimed at eleven to sixteen year old girls, while *Shoot* is produced for boys who are keen on football.

Every magazine has a style of its own. The publishers have to make sure that the **contents**, **design** and **language** of each magazine will appeal to the people they hope will buy it.

- The contents are all the different articles and features that are in a magazine. The contents page (usually at the beginning) lists all the articles and the page numbers where they can be found.
- The design of a magazine is its physical appearance. Design includes: size, how colour is used, headings (large or small), pictures (size, colour, subject matter, position), cartoons, and artistic bits and pieces (stars, stripes, zig-zags, etc).
- The language of the magazine should suit the audience. Are the articles easy to follow? Are they long or short? Are they broken up with headings? Is slang used? Or any technical words?

Look at the extracts below, taken from two magazines aimed at two very different groups of people. Notice how the two magazines differ in language, contents and design.

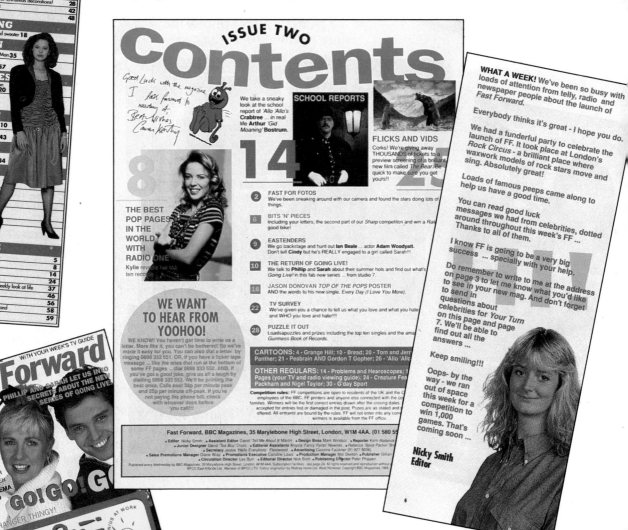

Prestige Publications are about to launch two new magazines. One is to help older people make the most of retirement, and is called *Enjoying Retirement*. The second one is called *Alive* and is a general interest magazine for eleven to fifteen year olds. The first issues of the two magazines are going to include articles and features on the following subjects:

Enjoying Retirement	*Alive*
money	clothes
cooking	films and videos
holidays	interviews with pop stars
gardening	television and radio
keeping fit	the latest crazes
letter page	competitions
book review	cartoons
	problem page
	horoscope
	newly released singles and albums

1   Design and produce the contents page for one of the magazines.

Give the articles and features eye-catching titles that will appeal to the readers. For example, the feature on holidays in *Enjoying Retirement* could appear as:

> ### Escaping From the Winter
>
> John Beardsley reports on inexpensive winter holidays in Spain and Portugal.

The feature on clothes in *Alive* could be set out like this:

> ### Fashion
>
> Get wrapped up in the brightest, warmest coats in the Cosmiverse!

2   To save money, Prestige Publications has decided to have the same editor for both magazines – *you*. As editor, you have to write an editorial of 150–300 words in each magazine to:

- welcome the readers to this new magazine;
- say how good the magazine is;
- draw the readers' attention to some of the articles and features in it;
- say that you hope the readers will enjoy it and buy it every fortnight.

BUT! Because you have been overworking, when you write the two editorials, you are so tired and confused that you write the editorial for *Enjoying Retirement* in the style of *Alive*, and vice-versa. Write the two editorials.

The language of magazines – compiling a glossary

In *Different kinds of English* (pages 7–41) you can produce a School Language Guide to help foreign visitors understand the different ways language is used in your school.

Foreign visitors would probably also need some help in understanding the comics and magazines you read because:

- the writing in them is informal and chatty;
- ordinary words are used in special ways;
- they contain new words that you wouldn't find in a standard dictionary.

1 In small groups, first make a list of the comics and magazines that you enjoy reading. Second, as you'll need a copy of five different comics or magazines to work on, decide which ones to use and who is going to bring them to school.

2 Go through the comics and magazines you've collected and pick out any words, phrases or complete sentences that a foreign visitor would have difficulty in understanding.

3 Write a helpful **glossary** of the words, phrases and complete sentences you have selected, explaining what each one means. For example

   wacky = unusual or weird

See Skills Session 12, What is a prefix? (page 175) and Skills Session 13, Verbs (page 176).

You can produce your own glossary and add it to your School Language Guide. You could also work together in groups or as a whole class, producing a glossary that could be displayed in the classroom along with the magazines and comics you have used.

focusing on experience

Contents

Introduction

In this Project, you are going to try out all sorts of ways of putting your experiences into words, and little by little you'll build up a complete portrait of your own world. This is quite a difficult thing to do – because there is no single best way of capturing real experiences truthfully and accurately.

It's like trying to take a single photograph of something – of someone's living room, for instance – so that you show exactly what that thing is really like. No one photo could do that – but if you took lots of different photos, from different angles and distances, using different light, and focus, and you looked at all the photos together – then you might begin to see what that room was really like.

Products

A **dossier** about your world. A collection of lots of different kinds of writing – all sorts of **snapshots** – that will show what the world you live in now, the world you know best at this stage in your life, looks like and feels like to you. So keep everything you produce in this Project.

Audience

Friends, relatives, neighbours, teachers – anybody who knows you and would like to find out more about you. But most of all, *you* – when you're grown up. It will be really fascinating to be able to look back and see the kind of person you were, the kind of things you did, the world you lived in, and what you thought about, when you were young.

1 Keeping an open diary

If you're writing a diary, it isn't possible to write down everything that happens in the course of a normal week: not every movement you make, every noise you hear, everything you eat or say, every time you wash your face, everything you see on television. You have to make a *choice*. You have to *select* what you think is worth remembering out of all the things that happen from day to day.

Keep an open diary of some of the most interesting and unusual things that go on in your everyday life, for using later on in the Project.

1 First of all, describe one *typical week* in your life at the moment. This will probably be a *school* week. Describe the things you normally do every week, going into detail about all the ordinary things that happen from day to day, like the example below.

> ## MONDAY
>
> 7.00 get up. Wash, dress quickly, eat cereals, toast with peanut butter and jam for breakfast. Feed gerbil. Complete homework. Leave to catch school bus by 8.10. Arrive school 8.35. Chat to friends. Registration 8.45. 9.00 first lesson - science. Sit with Karen. 9.45 second lesson - French. Sit with Nick. 10.30 break - eat packed lunch with Karen, Julie and Nick. 10.50 third lesson - maths. Sit with Julie. 11.35 fourth lesson - English. Sit with Karen, Julie and Nick. 12.20 lunch. Go to burger bar with Karen. Look at shops. 1.20 afternoon registration. 1.30 fifth and sixth lesson - double P.E. 3.10 end of school. 3.30 school bus leaves. 4.00 back home. 5.00 watch T.V. and have tea. 6.00 homework. 7.00 youth club. 10.00 go to bed. Listen to radio and read magazine. 11.00 go to sleep.

Because this is for work in school, you do not need to write down all the things that you might want to put in a *private diary* – this is going to be an *open diary*, so you must only write about things that you don't mind other people seeing.

REMEMBER – this is a normal or typical week in your life.

See Skills Session 15, Create the impression you want on page 180.

2 Next, under the heading OPEN DIARY – WEEK ONE start up a weekly record of special things that happen, and special things you do: interesting things, surprising things, annoying things, out-of-the-ordinary things.

Try to write in this diary every day for at least the next two weeks. Write a simple, brief description of anything out-of-the-ordinary or special that happens.

For example:

> <u>MONDAY 27th November</u>
>
> Overslept. Nearly missed school bus. Forgot maths homework. Nearly got detention. Teacher very sarcastic – not fair.
>
> Lunchtime – fight in burger bar!! Two fourth year boys started teasing a third year girl, who burst into tears. Bunch of five more third year girls came in and went for the two boys. Chased them round burger bar until manager threw them out. The girls chased the boys up the street. I think they got one of the boys, but the other escaped. Shame. Me and Karen helped the girl that had been teased to pick up her burger. Karen cleaned the dirt off it with her handkerchief – the girl didn't seem very pleased. Funny.

When you've completed week one of your open diary, make a start on the second week, under the heading OPEN DIARY – WEEK TWO, and so on, for however many weeks you do.

2 The world you know best

Landmarks

Write some *directions* that would take someone along the route you know best to where you live, that would show that person all the things – *the landmarks* – that you see every day as you go·to and from your home.

1   Choose a particular starting point for this journey, somewhere easy to find that is about ten or fifteen minutes walk from where you live:

- a bus or railway station,
- the town hall or village green,
- a war memorial or church,
- a cinema or supermarket,
- a crossroads or petrol station, etc.

It would help, of course, if this starting point is part of a route that you have often walked on your way home. Think about that route, and the places it passes.

> 2   Go on an imaginary walk in your head along this route,
> *from* the starting point you decided on
> *to* your home,
> *along* the paths and roads you know best.
> Really make your memory work.

Write down where you go, what you see as you pass by, and use these landmarks to explain where to turn left and right, or go straight on. Note down all the recognisable and interesting things that you notice as you go by, all the things that would help someone new to the area to find their way, all the things that are landmarks on your familiar landscape. These could be little things, like a bent parking meter or a broken gate, and big things like a bingo hall or a restaurant that always smells nice as you walk by.

> 3   At the next opportunity, actually do this walk yourself and take a notebook with you. See if:
>
> - you described the route accurately when you did that from memory;
> - you can pick out any other landmarks, large or small, which you realise, as soon as you see them, are also part of what you notice or glance at every day.
>
> 4   Write detailed directions for this journey, which would help someone else to:
>
> - find their way to where you live. Be clear about when to turn left and right, and how far to go each time;
> - recognise and see the important landmarks on the way.

For example:

> Start from the town hall, which is a great big grey building with the words TOWN HALL carved in a stone above the doorway. With your back to the town hall, cross over the town square, past the old green statue of a child on a horse until you see Marks & Spencers. There's often an old bloke playing an accordian by the entrance. Go down the street that runs along the front of Marks & Spencers, for about 200 metres until

> 5   If you get the chance, try out each other's routes using the directions that they have written, and look out for all the things they tell you to notice.

A room of your own

Whether or not you have your very own bedroom, or whether you share it with a brother or sister, you probably have a room that is partly yours – a place where you keep all your things and spend some of your time.

Imagine if you made a *display* out of your bedroom, so that someone could look in the door and see everything you own, and how your bedroom looks when you've got it just right, the way you like it best. That might be chaos, or it might be very well-organised.

1 Describe what someone would see if you had all your most familiar and favourite things, laid out for display in your room. You can do this from memory, or you can actually make a display of your room the way you want it, and then describe what you can see.
   Say where the different things come from, whether you're proud of these things or fed up with them, and perhaps what they reveal about you.

For example:

> *On the wall opposite the window there's a big poster of Bros that I've had for a couple of years now. I remember I persuaded my Gran to lend me a fiver to buy that, because I thought they were really great then. But I've grown out of them now.*
>
> *My cassette player, and a few cassettes are on the floor by the bed. I'm sick of all of them now, and mostly I just listen to the local commercial radio...*
>
> *My second favourite jeans are lying on the bed, next to my Dennis the Menace t-shirt. I'm sitting on the bed beside them, with my dog Neville next to me*

When you've finished this, you might perhaps be able to arrange for someone to take a photo of this scene, with you posing in the centre of the picture in your favourite clothes. You could stick this photo onto the bottom of your finished piece of writing.

2   Imagine, for a little while, that you are suddenly rich enough to have the room of your dreams, your ideal room.
What would it be like?
What things would you put on display – clothes, posters, books, objects?
Describe the things one would see if you made a display for a photographer of that room – of your ideal room.

Local characters

Describe three memorable local characters who play a big part in your daily life: a neighbour, friend, relative, the woman who runs the corner shop, a teacher . . .

In each case, describe the following things about this person:

■ who he or she is (e.g. friend, relative, shopkeeper);
■ what he or she looks like: how old, kind of hair, colour of eyes, the clothes they wear, what kind of face, etc;
■ what kind of person this is: friendly, grumpy, impatient, helpful;
■ what you think of this person.

Include in each description some very short story – an **anecdote** – about each of these people that is typical of what they're like, typical of the sort of thing they're always doing or saying.

3 Using reality in fiction

In 'The world you know best' (page 107), you concentrated on a lot of small details about the world you know best: the landmarks, possessions and people that are part of your daily life.

In this section, you are going to use all that detail for some **fictional** writing: the things that happen must be made up, but the setting, and the characters, can all be based on real places and people.

> 1   Write a short story (200–400 words). The things that happen must be completely *fictional*. The people, setting and physical details should be completely *real*.

This is a very short story, so you want what happens to be *simple*. Make up a story about something, or someone, being lost and found. This could be a possession that means a lot, or an animal, or a person. Make up most of what happens, although you might want to use something that once really happened as a starting point.

Make this fictional story happen to the real people that you know best, and make it happen in the real surroundings – the streets, and the rooms – that you know best. Include lots of detail about the objects and sounds that are part of your daily life.

Use the real names of the places and people you write about. It will be fun to move the real people you know around in the real places you know, and make them do whatever you want. Take care not to write anything *offensive* about anyone, though.

> 2   Write a long story (400–800 words). Again, you need to tell a *fictional* story using the real people, places and physical details that you know best, but this time you should *change* all the names of people and places.

What matters most is that you have real people and places in your mind as you write – but give everyone and everything *made-up names*. Use as much physical detail as you possibly can to describe the people and places you write about.

This long story should be about a misunderstanding:

- someone says something that gets misunderstood, and trouble begins;
- a misunderstood rumour starts to pass around, and trouble begins;
- someone misunderstands something they see going on in the distance, and trouble begins;
- someone is too shy to say or do what they really want, and trouble begins.

Don't write about *I* or *me* – write about *he* or *she*. Write about all your characters as if they were fictional – including yourself, if you are going to be in the story.

4 Different ways of writing about real life

Try out different ways of writing about something that really happened to you. See how things can change, when you write about them in four different ways:

1   story writing,
2   playscript,
3   tabloid newspaper front page,
4   photostory.

You will use the *same event* for each of these ways of writing.

First of all, you'll need to choose which event you want to use. Look back at the open diaries you have been keeping for the last few days or weeks. Choose *one event* that happened to you which is interesting enough to tell again, in different ways.

This doesn't have to be something very exciting, or dramatic – it can just be one thing that happened in your daily life that you remember well, and that you don't mind telling other people about. But it does need to involve more than one person, because you need to choose an event where people were talking to each other: you talking to your parents, or to friends, or teachers, etc. For example:

- going on a school visit,
- meeting someone new you really like,
- getting into trouble at school,
- playing well in a match,
- buying something special,
- having a row at home,
- going to a disco.

Talk about what happened with a fellow pupil.
Work in pairs for 10–15 minutes, and **interview** each other about the diary entry each has chosen.
Ask as many questions about exactly what happened: 'What did you do then?' 'What did she say?' 'How did you feel when that happened?'

The Burger Bar incident from 'Keeping an open diary' (page 106) will be used as an example of how one event can be written about in each of the four different ways that follow. This is how it was the first time:

MONDAY 27th November

Lunchtime - fight in burger bar!! Two fourth year boys started teasing a third year girl, who burst into tears. Bunch of five more third year girls came in and went for the two boys. Chased them round the burger bar until manager threw them out. The girls chased the boys up the street. I think they got one of the boys, but the other escaped. Shame. Me and Karen helped the girl that had been teased to pick up her burger. Karen cleaned the dirt off it with her handkerchief - the girl didn't seem very pleased. Funny.

If someone read you the Burger Bar incident as the event they had chosen from their open diary, you might ask questions like: 'Why were they teasing the girl?' 'What did they do to her?' 'What did she say?' 'What did you think when it happened?' 'What did you say?' 'Was the girl frightened?'

Once you have remembered as much as you can about what happened in the event you've chosen from your diary, you can go on to the first way of retelling it.

Story writing

The kind of story writing you will do here is **third person prose narrative**. That isn't as complicated as it sounds.

1 **Prose narrative** simply means the way you normally write stories (like the second story you wrote on page 111). In other words:

prose: writing continuously from margin to margin, *not* like verse;
narrative: telling a story from start to finish, explaining what happened, what people thought, and said.

You write prose narrative all the time – most of the stories you've ever written have been prose narratives, except for stories in verse, or playscript.

2 **Third person** means that the story you write seems to be about someone other than *yourself*.
Usually, when you tell a story about yourself, you write in a **first person** prose narrative. In order to turn a first person prose narrative into the third person, you simply change the *I*/*me*/*my* into *he*/*she*/*his*/*hers*.
That way, you can turn a diary entry into a story.

Before you begin to write your own third person narrative, look at this example – using the made-up story of the Burger Bar event as if it had been written by an imaginary pupil called Gill Watson:

It had been a typical Monday morning, and Gill couldn't wait to get out of school at dinner-time. She grabbed her mate Karen as soon as the bell went, and they set off for the town centre, and the old Burger Bar they always went to. It was a damp, foggy day and inside the Burger Bar the smell of fat and burnt buns was stronger than ever.

Gill and Karen liked it there. It was always crowded and lively, and it was a good place to meet their friends. That day, though, there was no one they knew well – just a couple of noisy fourth year boys, and a third year girl they vaguely knew, who was on her own. She was at the front of the queue, and she couldn't make up her mind about what she wanted.

'Er,' she was saying, 'can I have a quarter pounder without cheese for the same money as an ordinary burger *with* cheese?'

The boys were getting impatient, and began to bump into her, accidentally on purpose.

'No,' said the bloke serving. 'Quarter pounders is more. So what you having?'

'Come on,' yelled one of the boys.

'Get on with it,' muttered the other one.

The girl looked round at them, annoyed. 'Just wait a minute,' she said. 'Act your age.'

That seemed to make the boys even more impatient. They started whispering to each other, and Gill thought to herself that this looked like it was going to turn nasty in a moment. She was right.

Write about the event you have chosen from your open diary, in the same kind of way. Use plenty of dialogue.

Playscript

The Burger Bar Story could also be done as **playscript**. Look carefully at the example below, and notice how:

1   the **setting** for the incident – the **scene** – is described at the beginning;

2   most of the story is told through **dialogue** – what the characters say to each other;

3   **stage directions** are used to show what someone does or how they speak, for example: (*looking in her purse*) or (*whispering*);

4   the **layout** of the words:

 - no speech marks,
 - names of people speaking in CAPITALS,
 - stage directions in **brackets**,
 - new line every time someone begins to speak.

(Scene: a smelly old Burger Bar. Five schoolkids are queuing up to order burgers from a grumpy assistant behind the counter. A juke box is playing in the background. An old man is paying for his burger.)

GILL   What are you going to have today, Kar?

KAREN   (looking in her purse) Dunno – I haven't got much – can you lend us 20p?

GILL   Yeah, all right. *If* we ever get there.
(the two boys in front of them shove each other, and bump into the girl who has just gone up to the counter)

KAREN   Do you know her? (pointing to the girl at the counter)

GILL   Not really. I think her name's Tamsin. She's a third year, isn't she?

KAREN   (whispering, and pointing at the two boys) What about them?

GILL   I don't know *them* – wouldn't want to either.

KAREN   I reckon they're fourth years.

TAMSIN   (counting out coins in her hand) Er, can I have a quarter pounder without cheese for the same money as an ordinary burger *with* cheese?
(the boys bump into her again, harder this time)

ASSISTANT   No, quarter pounders is more. So what you having?
(girl looks blank)

BOYS   (both at once, shouting) COME ON! GET ON WITH IT!

KAREN   (whispering) Here comes trouble.

TAMSIN   Just wait a minute. (she raises her voice) *Act your age!*

GILL   She shouldn't have said that ...

Write your playscript version of your chosen event.
When you've written out your playscript, try acting out each other's finished versions, in small groups.

Tabloid front page

A **tabloid** newspaper is the small-sized kind of newspaper, like the *Sun* and the *Mirror*. Some tabloid papers try very hard to sell a lot of copies by making their front pages very sensational:

THE Sun

Thursday, December 21, 1989   22p   Audited daily sale for November: 4,000,992   Thought: Where is he?

GUESS WHO'S GOT A WIZARD NEW LOOK IN OZ, FOLKS? SEE PAGES 14 & 23

YANKS GO IN

WE'LL GET PINEAPPLE FACE

U.S. troops hunt tyrant

By EDDIE FITZMAURICE

PANAMA'S evil dictator Manuel Noriega was on the run last night after a bloody invasion by crack U.S. combat troops.

And a top American official promised: "We will chase him and we will find him."

Noriega, known as Pineapple Face because of his pock-marked features, fled before dawn as 24,000 U.S. troops struck to smash his corrupt regime in Central America.

Twelve Americans — including a civilian woman — and up to 60 Panamanians died in the fierce tank and artillery battles which raged through the night in Panama City and at military bases around the country.

There were also unconfirmed reports of 61 Americans taken hostage. Noriega's escape bitterly disappointed President George Bush.

He had gambled heavily by sending in the invasion force to seize the tyrant — wanted in America on drug charges — after a U.S. marine was shot dead in Panama at the weekend.

CAPTURE

And dismayed insiders at the Pentagon described the mission as a failure because Noriega, the main target of Operation Just Cause, had slipped through their grasp.

One official said: "In the final analysis it must be conceded that our

Continued on Page Two

On the run . .Panama dictator Manuel Noriega was being hunted by a U.S. invasion force last night

BLOWN TO OBLIVION: Pages 2 & 3 ● **20 THINGS ABOUT NUTTY NORIEGA:** See Page 4

Here is the Burger Bar story, told this time in the style of a tabloid front page:

BURGER RAMPAGE

Schoolkids torment pensioner

A ROMANTIC row between a 14 year old schoolgirl and two older boys sparked off a near-riot in a quiet market town yesterday.

Elderly pensioner, George Buckingham, who got caught up in the melee, commented afterwards, 'I was scared for my life. One moment I was eating my burger, the next thing I knew a gang of wild girls were beating up a couple of lads.'

Pleading

The fight is believed to have started as schoolkids were queuing up at lunchtime for their daily burgers. It just involved the girl and the two boys at first, says Burger Bar manager Clint King: 'I heard the boys pleading with this girl – come on said one, and make your mind up said the other. They obviously both wanted to go out with her.'

Suddenly, according to King, 'the place was full of angry schoolgirls,' and the boys ran out.

'It was great,' said schoolgirl Gill Watson, who is believed to be helping police with their enquiries. 'A real laugh.'

Beirut

Pensioner Buckingham, who is now under medication, commented, 'If that's how they get their laughs, I don't know what the world's coming to these days.'

This incident is just the latest in the current crop of teen outrages, presently making our country towns more like Beirut than Britain.

Tabloid front pages must be exciting.

Find out how to be a tabloid journalist by working on Skills Session 6 on page 164.

 Turn your story into a good tabloid front page story. Don't worry about sticking to the exact facts – just make it sensational!

Photostory

Finally, can you tell your story very simply, in just nine pictures? You should know the story pretty well by now – except that each time you tell it in a different kind of writing, the actual event you're telling about changes a bit.

Photostories must be easy-to-follow: they must set up a dramatic situation very quickly, and they need a strong, satisfying ending. The *end* is the important bit in a photostory, unlike real life – where things don't usually end neatly at all.

STAGE ONE: STORYBOARD

Draw a simple sketch version of the story, doing very basic matchstick-person drawings like the ones on the next page – just to show what should be going on in the pictures.

Make each box quite large, so that you can draw all the details you need. Work out what the characters are saying. You can give them quite simple dialogue – simpler than they would use in real life. Write them on small bubble shaped pieces of paper you can stick onto the drawings.

This is called a **storyboard**. It would show a photographer how to arrange the photos needed for a proper photostory. Here is a storyboard for the beginning of the Burger Bar story:

STAGE TWO: PHOTOSTORY

This will be much harder to do, of course, but it would be fun to do if you had the chance. Get hold of a camera, and set up the actual photographs in the way you planned them in the storyboard that you did for Stage One. You might need to use actors to play the parts of the real people who were originally involved. It would be interesting to see someone else acting you.

Here is some of the Burger Bar event, finally, told as a photostory:

5 Investigating your past

Images of childhood

What are very early memories *really* like? The earliest memories we have are usually not of complete events, or events that we know much about – they are usually images, pictures in our minds, that come back to us unexpectedly many years after they happened.

These images will probably be slightly unclear, like a photo with blurred edges and just odd details in focus, like: a face, a room, the sounds of a party, a piece of music, the smell of food, water and sky and sand, a road, a toy, an animal, a Christmas tree . . .

See if you can find any images from your distant past – just try to describe what is actually still in your memory. There's no need to fill in the gaps – to make up the things you don't remember.

Don't try to tell the exact story of any of these memories that you can recall – they might be like a single snapshot, or like a few brief moments of a film. Just name the things that flash in front of your mind's eye – like this description:

> I am sitting on someone's knee being fed with gruel. The plate is on grey oilcloth with a red border, the enamel white, with blue flowers on it, and reflecting the sparse light from the window. By bending my head sideways and forwards, I try out various viewpoints. As I move my head, the reflections in the gruel plate change and form new patterns. Suddenly, I vomit over everything.
>
> That is probably my very first memory.
>
> (Ingmar Bergman)

Describe some images from very early on in your life. You might not be able to describe them in as much detail as that extract, and they don't have to be first memories. You might be able to describe just bits from a snapshot in your mind – the image of a single moment. For example:

> ducks on a pond, a little boy crying, a piece of bread.

Or you might be able to describe a few moments from an event – like a short film. For example:

> Sitting around a dining table with brother and mother. The table is large and dark coloured. Father comes in and switches on the radio. 'Listen to this,' he says, laughing. We listen, and we all laugh.

Think about this to yourself for a while, and jot down whatever comes into your mind. The more you think about this, the more things you'll remember. Describe the images as you see them. Don't worry about writing proper sentences – just use words in whatever way best captures the things you see in your mind.

Your background

Ask the people who've known you for longest, the people who look after you – guardians, parents, step-parents, grandparents – about their memories of their own past. Try to interview at least two or three people.

Find out answers to the following questions, by interviewing them and looking at old photographs with them:

(questions for everyone)
- Where were you born?
- Where did you live when you were little?
- What was life like at home? Did you enjoy your childhood?
- What is the best memory of your childhood?
- Do you have any sad memories?
- What was school like for you?

(questions for grandparents)
- Was the world very different when you were young?
- What was mum/dad like as a child?
- Do you remember anything about the war?

It would be good if you could tape-record these interviews – that would make it easier to write down the most interesting things that they say afterwards. Otherwise, take careful notes while you are talking to them.

Write up your descriptions of the memories of each of these two or three people (and say something about any of the photos they show you that you find particularly interesting) as straightforwardly as you can. For example:

My grandmother - Mrs Dulcie Potter

My gran was born in Lowestoft in 1936. Her father was a fisherman, and they lived in a small cottage near the sea. She says that her earliest memories are of terrible storms blowing in from the sea...

If you are unsure how to do these two activities, turn to Skills Session 16, How to interview people, on page 181.

Memories of you

Interview people who knew you when you were very young –
parents, guardians, grandparents, elder brothers and sisters, aunts
and uncles, neighbours. Try to talk to several people, if you can.

Ask each person to tell you just one memory of you as a very young child
that sticks most clearly in their mind:

■ it might be very brief: maybe something as simple as the sight of you
  lying in a cot in hospital just after you were born;
■ it might be something funny, or something sad;
■ it might be something that was upsetting at the time, like a time when
  you were ill, or a moment when you were briefly lost.

It just needs to be something that means a lot to the person you're
interviewing.

Listen carefully to what each person says and ask any extra questions
about this memory that you want to know about. When you've
finished talking to each person, write down what they said as quickly
and simply as you can.

For example:

> *My mother says that when I was three I once got stuck halfway up a tree. I had . . .*

Autobiography

Autobiography means writing about your own life – in any way you want to.

- Why do people write about themselves?
- Why do we read other people's autobiographies?
- Is it possible to tell the truth about your own life?
- Is it possible to remember exactly what happened in your life, years and years later? If you wrote different versions of the same event in the previous section, you will know how difficult it is to remember what really happened, and what people really said only a few days earlier.

READING AUTOBIOGRAPHIES

> Look at the following extracts from three different autobiographies, each one remembering a story from the author's childhood:

1   The first extract is by Valerie Avery:

We children went to bed when it was still light outside and were allowed to talk quietly until Paul went to sleep, then we had to stop altogether otherwise he woke up and started bawling. That meant trouble for us and that was why Peter and I hated Paul. He always got in the way of our fun. Peter and I were about the same age. Paul was three years younger and was regarded by the grown-ups as the baby, the pet of the family. If one ice-cream cone was bigger than the rest, it was given to him, and he always had the treat of licking the rice tin or jelly bowl. But when we had him on our own, Peter and I got our revenge.

Up in the bedroom we tried to keep him awake by frightening him. One night I told him a story about the Man in the Moon. In my best creepy voice, I told him that 'there was a man who lived in the moon and he was very, very lonely. He wanted someone to keep him company, he wanted a little boy called Paul who was always sucking his thumb. One dark, frosty night, when the boy was fast asleep in bed, the man came down from the moon, climbed through the bedroom window and stole that little boy. Although Paul struggled to get free it was no use for the man only gripped him tighter and tighter and his fingers were not fingers but icicles that froze that little boy's heart. Higher and higher they went until they reached the moon. It was as cold as cold could be and Paul cried for his mother, but she couldn't hear him, nobody could hear him. And that poor little boy was never seen again.'

Paul was still having a fit of hysterics the following morning. He kept screaming out: 'Take the moon away! Take it way! He's coming after me! The moon! The moon!' Aunt Rose thought he was having a brainstorm and sent for the doctor. For weeks afterwards he had to stay indoors in a darkened room because if he saw the sky he became delirious. The grown-ups fussed over him more than ever, gave him everything he asked for, but at least Peter and I could play together in peace.

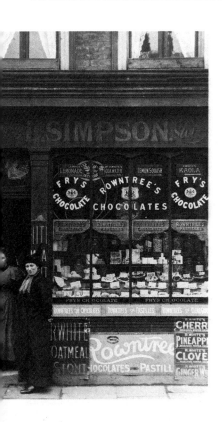

2   This extract is by Roald Dahl, from his autobiographical book *Boy*. It describes an incident when he was nine, involving a dead mouse and the hated Mrs Pratchett who ran the local sweetshop:

When writing about oneself, one must strive to be truthful. Truth is more important than modesty. I must tell you, therefore, that it was I and I alone who had the idea for the great daring Mouse Plot. We all have our moments of brilliance and glory, and this was mine.

'Why don't we,' I said, 'slip it into one of Mrs Pratchett's jars of sweets? Then when she puts her dirty hand in to grab a handful, she'll grab a stinky mouse instead.'

The other four stared at me in wonder. Then, as the sheer genius of the plot began to sink in, they all started grinning. They slapped me on the back. They cheered me and danced around the classroom. 'We'll do it today!' they cried. 'We'll do it on the way home! You had the idea,' they said to me, 'so you can be the one to put the mouse in the jar.'

Thwaites handed me the mouse. I put it into my trouser pocket. Then the five of us left the school, crossed the village green and headed for the sweet-shop. We were tremendously jazzed up. We felt like a gang of desperados setting out to rob a train or blow up the sherriff's office.

'Make sure you put it into a jar which is used often,' somebody said.

'I'm putting it in Gobstoppers,' I said. 'The Gobstopper jar is never behind the counter.'

'I've got a penny,' Thwaites said, 'so I'll ask for one Sherbet Sucker and one Bootlace. And while she turns away to get them, you slip the mouse in quickly with the Gobstoppers.'

Thus everything was arranged. We were strutting a little as we entered the shop. We were the victors now and Mrs Pratchett the victim. She stood behind the counter, and her small malignant pig-eyes watched us suspiciously as we came forward.

'One Sherbet Sucker, please,' Thwaites said to her, holding out his penny.

I kept to the rear of the group, and when I saw Mrs Pratchett turn her head away for a couple of seconds to fish a Sherbet Sucker out of the box, I lifted the heavy glass lid of the Gobstopper jar and dropped the mouse in. Then I replaced the lid as silently as possible. My heart was thumping like mad and my hands had gone all sweaty.

3   The third extract is again by Ingmar Bergman. He is describing a visit to the circus with his rich Aunt Anna, when he was seven years old:

This event drove me into a state of feverish excitement; the car journey with Aunt Anna's uniformed chauffeur, going into the huge brightly lit wooden building, the secret smells, Aunt Anna's voluminous hat, the blaring orchestra, the magic of the preparations and the roaring of lions and tigers behind the red draperies of the circus entrance. Someone whispered that a lion had appeared in the dark opening under the cupola and that the clowns were frightening and aggressive. I fell asleep from sheer emotion and awoke to wonderful music – a young woman dressed in white was riding around on a huge black stallion.

I was overcome with love for this young woman. She was included in my fantasy games and I called her Esmeralda (perhaps that was her name). My fiction finally took

an all-too-hazardous step out into reality. Under an oath of secrecy, I confided in the boy called Nisse who sat next to me at school. I told him that my parents had sold me to Schumann's Circus and I was soon to be taken away from home and school to be trained as an acrobat, together with Esmeralda, who was considered the most beautiful woman in the world. The next day my fantasy was revealed and desecrated.

My class teacher considered the matter so serious that she wrote an agitated letter to my mother. There was a dreadful court scene. I was put up against the wall, humiliated and disgraced, at home as well as at school.

On the cover of the Penguin edition of *Boy*, Roald Dahl says:

> *'Throughout my young days at school and just afterwards a number of things happened to me . . . Some are funny. Some are painful. Some are unpleasant . . . All are true.'*

Discuss all three extracts from these different writers' autobiographies, and consider the following questions about them:

- Do you think everything in them is accurate – do you think everything happened the way it is described?
- Which bits in them do you find most entertaining?
- Which bits in them seem most plain and straightforward?
- What matters most – to be completely accurate, or to entertain readers (even if that means making bits up or exaggerating a little)?
- Why do you think people write about themselves? Do you think it was important for these authors to tell these stories about their childhood?

WRITING AUTOBIOGRAPHY

You could probably write quite a long autobiography already. But for this Project, you are just going to write one story from your life so far.

In the course of this section, you will probably have recalled quite a few good stories about when you were much younger.

Choose your favourite story about yourself – something entertaining, or something that interests you particularly – and try to write it down in *two* different ways:

1   Write it as *accurately* as you possibly can. In other words:

- just say what you know for sure actually happened;
- explain about any bits you're unsure of;
- say how you know this story. Is it something you remember clearly? Is it something someone else has told you about yourself?

2   Write it as *entertainingly* or as *powerfully* as you can. In other words:

- think about ways of holding the readers' interest – by making it funny, or moving, or full of suspense;
- think about the ways this story can show how special and memorable your childhood really was.

You can use third person narrative for this (see page 114 of this Project if you're not sure what that is).

To help your writing, turn to Skills Session 17, Metaphors and similes on page 182.

6 Writing about who you are now

It's hard to recapture the past, and it's not easy to imagine the future, but it should be possible to say quite a lot about the present – and about the kind of person you are now.

1   Write down any thoughts that come into your head about at least five of the following things. In any way you want, as quickly and roughly as you like and without spending very long thinking about each one in advance, write a paragraph or two about each one you choose.

Nobody understands me
That's typical of me
My moods
The really good things about me
The people I admire most
The places I most want to go
The life I want to lead when I'm grown up
I wish I could afford . . .

My favourite meal
A perfect weekend
The kind of day I hate
What I like about school
Where I go when I want to be alone
The best thing that happened this year
My best friend

Look at the following letter:

11, Oxted Street
Northampton

June 11, 1992

Dear Cath,
    I hope you are well. I'm fine, though my knee is still a bit sore from when I fell off my bike. (remember that?).
    What are you up to nowadays? Are you living somewhere nice? Have you got computers that make the breakfast and clean the house while you're asleep? Have you got married? Did you decide to call the kids Jason and Kylie in the end? I hope you've got a good job. I'd like you to be an airline pilot, but a vet would be okay too. And what's the world like now? I hope they've saved the rainforests.
    How well do you remember ME? You probably can't remember what I was like, the things I enjoyed, the things that matter to me. I'm going to tell you some things about the way I am now.
    I am 13 years and 3 months as I write this and

...ke to stay at school if ...I'm sixteen and then I ...rsity or college.
...ring the summer we ...d it was really nice ...met a boy called ...es and a nice laugh. ...in Swansea though. ...ext year perhaps. ...it would hurry ...ke. I really wish ...ave a motor bike ...us. But Mum said ...wouldn't mind. ...etting back to me, ...t is happening to ...we to wait and ...u're reading this ...en you were 13.
...to wish you good luck in the future - I'm sure we'll have a great life.
                                    love,
                                        Cath.

2 Write a long letter to yourself, in the future. (This is the nearest to time-travel you'll probably ever get.)
Write to the person you're going to be in *twenty years time*. Tell this person, this future you, about you *now*: about the things you like to do, the things you want to do, about the kind of person you are now (the pieces you wrote under all those different headings in the last activity should help you a lot).

If you can, say something about how you see this future you, this person you'll be in your thirties – about the life you can imagine for yourself in twenty years time.

The example letter above will give you some ideas, but you must write this letter in the way you want to – so you don't have to follow the example closely unless that helps you to do this.

When you've finished this whole Project – *Focusing on experience* – and when your teacher has seen all the different things you've produced, and admired all the work you've done, and when you've shown it to all the other people who are interested in you:

3 Seal everything up in a big envelope, write your own name on the envelope, and an instruction not to open it for twenty years.

For example:

> *to Cathy Williams*
>
> NOT TO BE OPENED UNTIL 2012

It will be very exciting, when the day finally comes, to take that envelope from the safe place you will have stored it for all those years (without cheating, and reading it ahead of time) and to open it up and read all those different things that you wrote and thought when you were young.

You really ought to include a photo of you as you are now – perhaps the one of you sitting in your own room, if you have that.

Most of all – it will be very exciting to read the letter from *yourself* – the letter you wrote all those years before.

influencing people

Contents

Introduction

When you learn to do things with language, you are learning to deal with the world. When you study English, you find out about how language can help you make sense of the world, get on in the world, and change the world.

The word *world* can mean the place where you spend most of your time, your home. It can mean the world of people, jobs, entertainment, politics. And it can mean the *whole, wide world*. However you use it, world means all that is important in life. When you learn to use language successfully, you learn to deal with the world successfully.

This Project is about just that – using language to make your voice heard in the world, and to help make the world a better place. Language can influence people. Language is powerful, and you have the right to use it powerfully. In this Project, you're going to learn some ways of doing that.

Products

The final products of this Project will be campaign materials – carefully argued essays, helpful leaflets, dramatic posters – that might influence a lot of different people.

Audience

The outside world – friends relatives, the general public and, perhaps, some of the people who make important decisions in life.

1 Getting people to take notice of you

Using appropriate language

Dear Sir,

Sit! Steady now, that's good, relax. DON'T MOVE! Right, right.

I am quick on my feet – DON'T MOVE – and love all animals. Steady now. I have a STRONG VOICE, and even my Dad does what he's told when I'm around. DOWN!

I am writing to apply for the post of lion-tamer in your circus. Don't move, STAY! Just give me the job, NOW! Good boy, well done.

Yours forcefully,
C. Brown

Dear Sir,

I'm sorry to disturb you, sir. I was just wondering if you would care to consider my application for the job of waiter/waitress in the exclusive and expensive Restaurant de Paris, advertised in today's 'Times'.

Please may I tell you a little about myself? I hope you will find something to your taste.

I am well-mannered and extremely polite. I am small and neat. The customers would hardly notice me, I assure you, I am so quiet and respectful. I have a good memory, a good sense of balance, and I am quick on my feet. I am sure that I will be to your liking, sir.

Please consider this application for as long as you wish, and let me know when you are ready to give me your order.

Thank you very much for your kind attention.

Yours patiently,
C. Brown

> Write a short letter of application for three of the following jobs – one of these should be for number 5, an assistant in Prince Charles' office. As the examples above show, these applications will not be exactly what you would write in a normal job application.

Choose your words with care, to present yourself as the kind of person you think would be wanted, in each case.

1   The lead singer in a heavy metal band. What *image* would you need to present? How do tough, trendy and cool rock-singers use words?

2   A soldier in the army. You'll need to be straight-talking, snappy, not the kind to waste words, and well disciplined.

3   Someone to write the rhymes for greetings cards, things like:

> *Hope it won't be long before*
> *You're up and out of bed*
> *With nothing but the best of health*
> *And happy days ahead.*

4   The presenter of a new television youth show. You'll need to demonstrate an ability to use language smoothly and confidently without pausing, and to be excited about *everything*.

5   An assistant in Prince Charles' office. Prince Charles once complained that 'All the people I have in my office, they can't speak English properly and they can't write English properly.' So you'll have to be very careful about the way you write this one.

See Skills Session 20, Choose the right words for the job, page 186.

House-rules

Imagine you were living in a house with a few other people like yourself. Five or six of you – all trying to get on in one home together, no one in charge, everyone deciding together how to do things.

- How important would it be to you to keep the place clean and tidy?
- What arrangements would you have for preparing food?
- Who would decide what you watched on television?
- How would you avoid annoying each other?

1   Write the house-rules *you* would want people to follow:

- so that people didn't annoy each other,
- spoil each other's fun, or
- disturb each other's peace.

These rules might be about very small things, like the way people treat the toothpaste tube, or important things, like how people treat each other.

Write the rules that you would like people to follow in the house you shared.

2   In a group of five or six, *agree* on a set of house-rules. This will not be so easy.

Imagine you are all living in the same house together – five or six very different people, who don't necessarily know each other or even like each other very much.

- What are the house-rules you could all accept, and keep to?
- Argue the case for the house-rules you would want.
- Listen to what each of the others want.
- Work out the rules that every one of you can accept. Write down what you decide.

3   In your same group, act out a short improvised drama about life in this imaginary household that you all share, with its agreed set of house-rules.

This could take place either at breakfast time with everyone half-awake and irritable, or during a typical evening in the house – with people trying and sometimes failing to follow the rules you've agreed.

As usual, things go wrong, and people begin to argue. Everyone has probably got a lot to say – complaints about rules that are being broken, complaints about having to follow unnecessary rules, suggestions for change or improvement to the rules.

Everyone has the right to say what they think.

4   As a group, design a poster to be displayed in the entrance to the house, stating just *three* simple rules that everyone using the house should follow: simple, unfussy rules that make life easier for everyone.

The poster should be eye-catching, easy to understand, and easy to remember. It should be something that helps everyone to treat each other *fairly*.

Are you getting a fair deal?

Read these two letters sent by young people to *The Indy*, about things that they think are unfair:

We're all the same inside

BEING GREEK I have been called many names, although I don't take them seriously. For example, I have been called "Greasy Greek". What is the difference between people of light skin and people with darker skin? They all have feelings and are exactly the same inside.

Iliana Taliotis, 12

We are people – not animals

I FEEL very strongly about the way that adults treat children of about the five-to-fourteen-year-old age range

These adults are usually not parents, otherwise they would understand the child's feelings. The offending adult cares only for their own welfare and does not consider the child's point of view or rights.

If an adult pushes past you or is served first in a queue and you protest, the adult's immediate reactions are either to ignore you or to let you past with many a "Tut! Such rudeness!"

Adults who would never even dream of stepping on one another's toes, drop cigarette ash in your hair or fell you with shopping bags.

Others treat you like animals – in fact, I distinctly heard one woman say to another as they tried to get past me, "Oh, push on, Nicole. Get past it, for Pete's sake!" I think it was the "it" that hurt me most. Now, the climax of my complaint.

Of course I am concerned about the ozone layer, pollution and poaching, but up there with all those other problems are the rights and treatment of children by the adult world.

Charlotte Edwards, 12

- Do you think your life is fair? Are some people having a better time than you? Are you having a better time than other people?
- Do you live in the countryside? lovely green fields? fresh air? peace and quiet? no buses? no cinemas? no shops? nothing to do?
- Do you live in a city? lots of shops, cinemas, sports facilities? lots of noise, pollution, poor housing?
- Do you belong to a group in society that is treated badly? Do adults treat you badly? Do other kids treat you badly?
  What have *you* got to complain about?

1 Discuss this as a class. Discuss the kinds of things that people have got to complain about, in their lives. You might only want to talk about small irritations, or you might want to talk about things that are extremely important.

Just follow these two rules:

- Tell the truth – don't exaggerate, don't hold back.
- Let others tell the truth – listen to what they have to complain about, and don't make fun of them.

> **2** Write a letter, complaining about whatever you think is most unfair in the way you, or other people you know about, are treated. Come right out and say what you think.

Just one rule this time:

REMEMBER THAT EVERYONE, INCLUDING YOU, HAS THE RIGHT TO BE TREATED FAIRLY.

As long as you write nothing that breaks that rule, you can write whatever you think – as clearly, and strongly, as you like.

Write a **first draft** quickly, straight on to the page. If you feel angry about the things you're writing about, say so.

Swap your writing round with each other, and comment on what each other has written. If you read something that ignores, or breaks, the rule that 'everyone, including you, has the right to be treated fairly' talk about that, and suggest ways of changing it.

If someone writes something that really annoys you, write a reply. Listen to what anyone says about your writing, and think about ways of making it fairer if necessary.

If necessary, if you think the first draft can be improved, write a **second draft**.

If you think that you, and your fellow pupils, have written important things, then make sure that other people read them, either by making them into displays or booklets.

No one has something important to say *all* the time. If what you wrote didn't turn out right, just throw it away and try again when you do feel strongly about something.

To improve your writing, turn to Skills Session 17, Metaphors and similes, on page 182.

2 An imaginary campaign

DAILY HARD LINES

JANUARY 1st, 2001

Speak Proper – Or Else!

YESTERDAY a new law came into force requiring everyone below the age of 16 to speak properly at all times.

From today, it is now against the law for young people EVER to use slang, local accents, and incorrect English.

This law is an important part of the government's drive to improve the general behaviour of young people, which had got completely out of control by the end of the twentieth century.

Said Terence Knight, prime minister and leader of the ruling Strict Party coalition: 'No longer will we have to put up with youngsters talking sloppily, dropping their aitches, and using slang words that nobody can understand.'

This follows the recent laws requiring young people to dress nicely and go to bed by 8.30 every night.

'This language law will be as unpopular as all the others,' said recently appointed Language Inspector Cindy Strong yesterday. 'But we don't expect young people to be capable of doing much about it, so there won't be any big problems.'

This is an imaginary news story about an imaginary event. It hasn't happened yet, and it probably never will. But human beings have done far worse things to each other than this before now, so it isn't *impossible*.

Imagine how you'd feel if this really did happen and you weren't allowed to say things like:

dunno	*dead good*
innit?	*done a runner*
wotcha	*telly*
'orrible	*ol' slap'ead*

What if you were not allowed to use your local accent, or shout out what you liked at matches, or talk to your friends in your own way?

Discuss whether or not you think a law like this would be fair. Consider these questions.

- How would you feel if you had to change the way you spoke?
- Who should decide how you speak?
- When is it all right to speak informally and casually?
- When do we need to speak formally, and politely?
- How would you argue *for* a law like this?
- How would you argue *against* it?

Newspaper editorials

Newspaper editorials are different from news stories. They don't try to give you the *facts* about what happened. They just give you the newspaper's *opinion* about something. Look at this example from *Today* newspaper:

Open season

A YEAR after pubs were allowed to stay open through the day there is nothing to report except satisfaction.

Pubs have simply adjusted to the needs of their customers. Some stick to the old hours, some take full advantage of the new. The mayhem predicted just has not happened.

The same, we predict, would be the case if shops were allowed to open on Sundays. Some would and some wouldn't. But Sunday would still be Sunday after all.

The Government should use the precedent of the pubs to push again for Sunday opening. Mrs Thatcher knows it makes sense.

Editorials are just *opinions*. It's up to you whether or not you agree with them. In this example, the paper is saying that the Sunday trading laws should be changed, so that people could do what they liked on Sundays. The paper has the right to say that, and you have the right to disagree.

Write two editorials about the news story in the *Daily Hard Lines*:

- one written by an editor who thinks the new law is wonderful, and who wants to convince the readers to think the same;
- the other written by an editor who strongly disapproves of the new law, and thinks it is unfair.

Make each editorial short and sharp – no more than 75 words. Each one can give just one good reason for their opinion. Your editorial should discuss the news story, and not tell it.

Using language to protest

Mount an imaginary campaign against this imaginary law. Try out some of the ways you can use language to stand up for your rights.

> 1   Write a letter to your Member of Parliament, asking for her or his support in Parliament to change the new law.

What kind of letter should you write? What **tone of voice** is most likely to make someone important and influential like an MP listen to what you have to say? You could be:

- *aggressive and angry*, making it quite clear how stupid you think everyone in Parliament is;
- *flattering and apologetic*, trying to win her or him over with sweet words;
- *indifferent and reasonable*, as if all this was nothing to do with you;
- *firm, committed, but calm*, saying what you think, and what you want, without being rude – so that the MP can't ignore your letter straight away.

Each of you try to write a letter. Read each other's letters, and see what tone of voice comes across. Discuss each other's letters, and whether they use the most appropriate tone of voice for this particular purpose.

Rewrite your first version if you now think the tone of voice isn't appropriate. As a class, read out your finished letters, and discuss which ones would be most likely to work best, and why.

> See Skills Session 19, How to write formal letters (page 184)
> and Skills Session 20, Choose the right words for job (page 186).

2   Design a simple, powerful poster.

The aim of a poster is to make people aware of your cause, so that they will support you. You want people to notice what you're trying to say, and to think about it.

Look closely at these three Oxfam posters.

All three posters create their effect by using a simple combination of a **visual image** and a simple **slogan**.

It only takes a moment to find out what the posters are about, whether it's wastefulness in our own society, or pollution, or the injustice of poverty. Posters should make their point very simply, quickly, immediately.

The most important things that a good poster needs to do are:

■ look good – it should force people to look at it;
■ be simple and memorable – once people have seen it, it should stay in their minds.

What will you need to include in your poster?

■ It will be about young people being treated unfairly by adults.
■ It will be about the language that young people should be allowed to use.

Will it be more effective to use slang, or very formal language, in your slogan? That's a difficult question, which only you can answer by designing your poster, and trying out different ideas.

3   Make a speech.

'Friends, Romans, and countryman – lend me your EARS!'

Write a speech that you could make to a crowd of supporters. The purpose of this speech will be to work up a mood of enthusiasm and excitement. The people you'll be talking to will mainly be on your side. So this speech won't be attacking them – it will be bringing them all together.

A speech like this doesn't need to go on very long. It should just make two or three points in a forceful and rousing way, so that when it's finished, people go off wanting to do something about your cause.

It should use some of the tricks of speech-making that expert speech-makers know about – ways of using language that make people applaud, and feel excited.

To find out more about how to do this, go to Skills Session 21, How to make speeches, on page 188.

The main points you will try to make in this speech would probably be:

- *state the fact* that there is this new law about how young people can speak, and it's unfair;
- *demonstrate the fact* that the new law is absurd and silly – try to show how it will make young people sound unnatural and ridiculous;
- *persuade people* that they should join together and protest against it.

If you can, try out the speech you write on your fellow pupils and find out how well the tricks you've used actually work.

Happy ending

Your campaign has been a complete success!

Write the front-page newspaper article for the *Daily Hard Lines*, on June 1st, 2001, telling readers that the government has decided to end this law, and explaining how the young people's campaign against the law achieved this brilliant success.

3   Are you turning green?

Friends of the Earth

What's happening to the earth?

- Over 130 million trees are cut down every year to provide us with paper and board. The average British family of four threw away six trees' worth of paper in 1987.

- Every minute of every day, an area of tropical rainforest the size of 200 football pitches is destroyed.

- Humankind uses an amount of fossil fuel in one year that it took nature roughly a million years to produce.

- Forests absorb carbon dioxide (CO_2). When they are cut down and burnt, more CO_2 is released into the atmosphere, and less is absorbed. This leads to the Greenhouse Effect – the increased CO_2 in the atmosphere slows down heat loss from the sun, and the earth's average temperature gradually rises a tiny bit. If this happens for much longer, the polar ice-caps will begin to melt, putting large areas of the earth under water. Other parts of the earth will become too hot, turning essential farm land into desert.

- Nearly 4½ billion drink cans were thrown away in Britain during 1986.

- It takes 500 years for a disposable nappy to decompose.

- One of the basic laws of nature is that nothing actually disappears when it is thrown away.

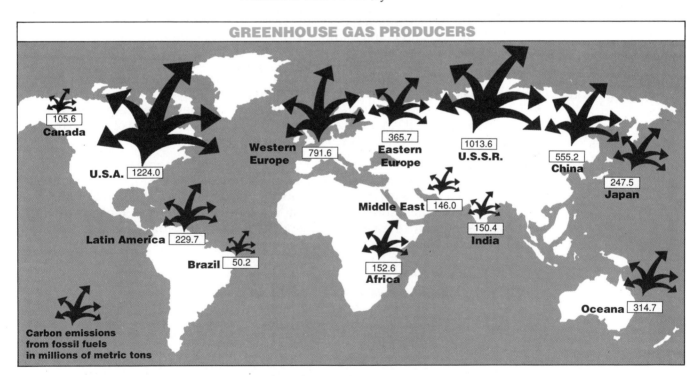

GREENHOUSE GAS PRODUCERS

105.6 Canada
U.S.A. 1224.0
Western Europe 791.6
Eastern Europe 365.7
U.S.S.R. 1013.6
China 555.2
Japan 247.5
Middle East 146.0
India 150.4
Latin America 229.7
Brazil 50.2
Africa 152.6
Oceana 314.7

Carbon emissions from fossil fuels in millions of metric tons

The map shows how much carbon dioxide pollution is being kicked up into the atmosphere. The effect of this is not fully predictable. The earth has been here for aeons. We are very much newcomers.

'Planet Earth is 4,600 million years old. If we condense this time span to an understandable concept, we can liken the earth to a person 46 years of age. Dinosaurs did not appear until a year ago. In the middle of last week, man-like apes appeared. Modern man has been around for four hours.

During the last hour man discovered agriculture. The industrial revolution began a minute ago. In 60 seconds of biological time, Modern Man has made a rubbish tip of paradise. Now he stands like a brutish infant, on the brink of destroying this oasis of life in the solar system.'

- Every year about 3½ million tonnes of oil are released into the oceans.

- Chemicals in aerosol sprays and fridges are fast destroying the ozone layer. This layer of the earth's atmosphere protects us from harmful rays of the sun. Without it, we are in greater danger of getting skin cancer.

- Twenty years ago there were 3 million elephants in Africa. Now there are about 700,000.

- In 1970 there were 20,000 rhinos in Kenya. Today there are only 450 rhinos left.

- About 45 million chickens are kept in crowded battery cages, and 450 million animals are killed for food in this country every year.

How do you feel about this?

In the last few years, green issues have been constantly in the news. People are beginning to believe that our planet, and all that lives on it, is in danger, and that they must do something about that before it's too late.

It is not too late *yet*. It's your world. You have the right to a healthy world for you and your children. You also have the right to demand that it is looked after properly.

Of course, you might not want to do much about green issues either because you've heard enough about them already to last you a life-time, or because you think there are other equally important issues to deal with. But it's hard to argue with the fact that the future of the earth matters to you as much as it matters to everyone else.

If, at the end of this Project, you decide to ignore green issues for a while, that's fair enough and quite understandable. Few people can spend all their time worrying about how to save the earth. But if you decide to ignore them forever, you won't find them going away. Unless you find some way of leaving this planet for a safer one, you're going to have to think about the environment quite often.

Discuss your attitude to green issues:
- What do you feel about the future of the planet?
- What do you feel about doing something about it?

What can you do?

1   You can find out what's going on. You can find out the *facts* by reading, watching, listening and learning.

2   You can *join forces* with others to improve things, in your home, your street, your school, your town, and your world by communicating with people, mounting campaigns, and making your voice heard.

How? You can use the *power of language* to do all these things.

Read this extract from a long article in the *Observer*, and the two short items that follow it, which suggest ways that ordinary people can help stop greenhouse gases escaping into the atmosphere, and can help to save the environment.

> As you read, note down any suggestions that you think sound useful, and possible to do something about.

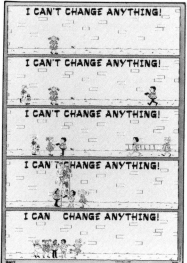

Imagine a typical Saturday. We wake and turn on the light. Most electricity is generated by burning coal and oil, which give out carbon dioxide. The common light bulb is an incandescent one, which uses 80 per cent more electricity than the less common compact fluorescents. As with most anti-greenhouse actions, we also end up paying less – in this case, on the electricity bill.

We stumble to the kitchen to make breakfast. Here is a most fruitful area for carbon dioxide savings. The energy efficiency of different brands of kitchen appliances varies a lot. Huge savings can be made by choosing the right kind of freezer, fridge and kettle. When it's time to buy a new appliance, anti-greenhouse citizens should ask about the energy-efficiency of products before they buy.

If it's a cold day, many people will have been burning up a lot of precious energy in heating their homes – energy which could be saved by insulating their homes more efficiently. In Finland, electricity bills can be as low as £20 per year in super-insulated homes, despite the freezing weather. In the long run, good insulation saves money – but it does cost money to put it in the first place, which can be a problem.

We read our newspaper as we unwrap our breakfast cereal from layers of paper packaging. In most households, all this will go in the bin, to find its way eventually to a landfill dump. There it will decompose, producing methane – a greenhouse gas 25 times worse than carbon dioxide when it comes to heating the atmosphere. The methane in the atmosphere is growing at 1 per cent a year – tens of millions of tonnes annually – is seeping from rubbish tips. So greenhouse-conscious citizens recycle their paper and do not bother with packaging in the first place. Many health and wholefood stores will pour cereals direct into re-usable bags.

Next stop is the shops. Most people go by car. The average car produces nearly four times its body weight in carbon dioxide each year. In the UK, our cars manage an average of 30 miles to the gallon. The best available model does 57 mpg. Many current prototypes can achieve between 70 and 100 mpg – one Renault has achieved 124 mpg in trials. Anti-greenhouse citizens will choose their next model with these figures in mind. They also share their cars more and use public transport where possible. Some

15 per cent of global carbon dioxide emissions come from cars and light vans. The scope for savings is phenomenal. If the United States improved the fuel efficiency of its average vehicle from 17 to 30 mpg, it would not need to import oil.

Once at the shops, there are several choices available to the anti-greenhouse citizen. We can begin by avoiding all aerosols propelled by chlorofluorocarbons. CFCs are 10,000 times worse as greenhouse gases than carbon dioxide and they also attack the protective ozone layer.

We should also avoid any product made of tropical hardwood, and look for the Friends of the Earth 'good wood' seal. This is a small but vital step in preserving rain forests, whose destruction contributes up to 40 per cent of all carbon dioxide emissions.

Organic food is also greenhouse-friendly. Nitrous oxide, a gas produced when fertilisers are added to the soil, is a greenhouse gas. The more people who buy organic food, the more the prices will be reduced and the more organic farming – anti-greenhouse farming – will be encouraged.

Next stop, the meat counter. The world's cattle produce about 100 million tonnes of methane each year. Anti-greenhouse citizens should eat far less meat.

From here, anti-greenhouse opportunities for the individual move from consumerism to activism. If you're worried about global warming, you can write letters to influential people. Encourage your local council to use recycling schemes. Get them to plant trees and tap the methane from dumps to heat buildings. Co-ordinated lobbying of businesses, seeking proof of anti-greenhouse production processes, as well as greenhouse friendly products, will surely influence what they plan to do in future.

Seven ways to save the world

1 Cut pollution from cars by raising fuel efficiency and fitting catalysts to mop up exhaust gases that cause acid rain and smogs.

2 Cut coal and oil-burning emissions of carbon dioxide, the main greenhouse gas, by 20 per cent by the year 2005 — a realistic target if energy efficiency were stimulated by a global carbon tax.

3 Establish a global fund to pay for poor countries to develop their economies using clean technologies.

4 Halt the destruction of rain forests. The forests slow the greenhouse effect and keep the planet cool by recycling rainwater.

5 Tackle the world's waste mountain by recycling everything from bottles to toxic industrial wastes.

6 Use people power — in the supermarket, at the ballot-box and through the power of protest.

7 Persuade economists, bankers and governments to use taxes and accounting methods to ensure that the polluter pays.

The following two items from the same edition of the *Observer* suggest other things that can be done:

Your dustbin: The inside story

EVERY year the average Briton dumps one-third of a tonne into the rubbish bin. In paper alone, the average household throws away six trees' worth annually. End to end, the 4,450 million drinks cans disposed of in the UK in 1986 would reach the moon.

☐ Friends of the Earth estimate that we could recycle at least 50 per cent of our rubbish, almost all of which is bound for a landfill. This is a breakdown by weight of what we throw away:

☐ Kitchen waste — 30 per cent. Much could be recycled in a compost heap, large-scale or as compact as an adapted dustbin. The resulting mixture can be used for potting plants, as fertiliser or, dried, as cat litter.

☐ Paper — 25 per cent. A first step would be to use less by stopping junk mail (contact Mailing Preference Service, Freepost 22, London W1E 7EZ for details) and any unwanted free newspapers, re-using envelopes and writing on both sides of sheets. While there are good markets for cardboard and letter-quality paper, newspapers and magazines are the main concern. Call your council or local Friends of the Earth to find the nearest collection point. Consumers can strengthen the market by buying recycled writing paper, envelopes and even toilet paper.

☐ Textiles — 10 per cent. Clothes can be taken to a charity shop, some of which accept rags and old woollens.

☐ Glass – 10 per cent. There are 3,850 public bottle banks now. If you think more are needed in your area, lobby the council or local supermarkets.

☐ Metal — 8 per cent. Tins and cans are recycled by Save-a-Can skips or through the Aluminium Can Recycling Association's 'recycling centres' at scrap metal dealers. In addition, some authorities magnetically extract tin plate cans from refuse to be recycled. Some drinks brands, such as 7-Up, identify all-aluminium cans with an 'alu' symbol. Others do not, but you can test any can by putting a magnet on its base: it will not stick to aluminium. For more information, contact the association on 021-633 4656.

☐ Plastics — 7 per cent. Almost no plastics are recycled in Britain except in pilot schemes.

☐ Dust, ashes and other materials — 10 per cent.

Discuss the different suggestions made in these *Observer* items, and see if you can choose at least five things that it's worth trying to persuade people to do.

Few of these things can be done by one person alone but a lot can be done if lots of people try to change things together.

The first thing to do is to convince people that green issues are important, and are not just a passing fashion – unless, of course, the earth itself is a passing fashion.

Design a poster which convinces people of two points:

- that the earth is in danger, and needs protecting;
- that they should try just one of the five ways of protecting the earth you found out about in the items from the *Observer*.

On the other hand . . .

Use some of the facts on the previous pages to write a calm and reasoned essay about the arguments *for* and *against* worrying about the environment.

The argument *for* worrying about the environment will need to use several of the facts you have come across already, which warn us about the dangers that the planet is facing. You can also include any other similar facts that you know, that you think are important.

The argument *against* worrying about the environment could include points like:

- now that life has become convenient and comfortable, the green movement want to stop us enjoying ourselves, by stopping us eating the things we like and doing convenient things like travelling by car;
- worrying about green issues makes us forget about other things, like world poverty, unemployment, sexism, racism and old people.

Discuss both sides of the argument for worrying about the environment, and end the essay by saying which side you find most convincing. Call the essay 'Do we really need to turn green?'

If you really are interested . . .

You can join an environmental organisation like Friends of the Earth:

Dear Friends Of The Earth

Can I please become a member of Friends Of The Earth. Or something like that. So I can raise money for you to help the environment. Because I'm very worried about the greenhouse effect, the rainforest being cut down, nuclear power and waste, the hole in the ozone problem, river and sea pollution and leaded petrol. Please can you give me this information. Thank you.

from
Andrew Powers
Age 11½

'For some time now, Andrew has been concerned about green issues and he keeps up to date by watching environmental programmes on television. He and his friends at St Catharine's School, Ware, are particularly worried about the greenhouse effect and Andrew is now thinking of ways to raise money to help FoE's work in this area.'

 You can also find out if you can join an organisation like Friends of the Earth (FoE) – as a group, or class.

4 Running real campaigns

You are going to try out some ways of running a real campaign. You will:

- *think about* some campaigns you could actually run;
- *practise* some of the ways of using language you would need for any effective campaign.

Then, possibly, you might actually run a real campaign – but only if you really want to do that. It wouldn't be good for anyone if you started a campaign that you didn't mean to follow through.

Ideas for campaigns

These campaign suggestions are all about improving the quality of people's lives in your local area – by:

- *either* conserving just a few of the earth's resources and improving the environment where you live;
- *or* looking after the right of yourselves and others to lead a safe and fair life.

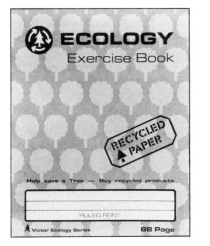

CAMPAIGN ONE: USING PAPER WISELY IN YOUR SCHOOL

In Britain, each one of us uses up an average of 130 kg of paper every year – that's about 1½ trees each per year. Paper products use up roughly 35 per cent of the world's annual wood harvest, and the figure is still rising.

Instead of cutting down more trees all the time, we could *waste* less paper, and we could re-use our waste paper – *recycle* it. At present only a quarter of the world's paper is recycled – it would be possible to double that amount during the next ten years. *If we wanted to.*

- How much paper do you use every week?
- How much paper does your school use each year? each day?
- How much money is spent on paper by your school each year?
- What ways can you think of to stop people wasting paper?
- How much paper, and money, do you think could be saved in your school?
- Can you persuade the school to buy and use recycled paper?

A successful campaign should aim to:

1 collect lots of useful facts about the way people use paper in your school, and what the cost of all that is;

2 figure out ways of stopping people wasting paper unnecessarily;

3 argue the case to convince the people in charge about the need to save paper, and of ways of doing that;

4 find out about opportunities in your area for collecting and selling waste paper for recycling;

5 argue the case to convince the people in charge to use recycled paper, and collect waste paper if possible;

6 publicise the campaign to save paper, use recycled paper, and collect waste paper.

£24,000
TO BE COLLECTED

CAMPAIGN TWO: RECYCLING RUBBISH

A really exciting way of finding out facts in this campaign would be to empty out your dustbin and see what's in there. This would be exciting because you'd probably end up in the dustbin yourself, if you got caught.

For this campaign, turn back to 'Your dustbin: the inside story', the item from the *Observer* on page 149 of this book. It outlines several very useful things you can do with your household rubbish, which will help protect the environment in the long-run, especially if you can get lots of other people to do the same things.

Look, too, at the advert at the top of this page.

All you need is a magnet and a pile of cans – the ones that don't stick to the magnet are the aluminium ones.

A successful campaign would aim to:

1   identify the things that can be done in your local area to recycle rubbish (you'll need to write to your local council or Friends of the Earth to find out what local schemes already exist);

2   persuade your local council to start up recycling schemes, if they don't have any already;

3   use posters and leaflets to publicise ways of recycling rubbish.

CAMPAIGN THREE: TRANSPORT

Nearly 40 per cent of all journeys in Denmark are done on bicycles. In Britain the figure is nearer 4 per cent. Cyclists are not well-looked after in this country. Fourteen year-old boys are most at danger on bicycles, but all young people on bicycles are at risk.

The most dangerous thing to do on a bike is turning right – but there are all sorts of dangers on the roads for cyclists: parked cars, badly lit streets, complicated crossroads and traffic lights, holes in the road.

And it's not all that much safer to walk.

- How dangerous are the roads for young people where you live?
- What are the particular problems for young cyclists?
- What are the particular problems for young pedestrians?
- Where are the danger areas?

A successful campaign should aim to:

1 find out about the particular dangers on the roads where you live;

2 find out about local road safety schemes – like 'Safe routes to school';

3 argue the case for improvements to the roads;

4 publicise the need to use roads more safely.

CAMPAIGN FOUR: FACILITIES FOR THE DISABLED

Disabled people have as much right to move around and take part in life as everyone else. But they often find that very few facilities are provided for them: poor public transport, inadequate public conveniences, shops which they can't go into with wheelchairs, fire safety rules which keep wheelchairs out of many cinemas and theatres.

Most schools were not designed with disabled people in mind, so that they often have to go to special schools. They are made to believe that they don't belong in the same world as able-bodied people, and many able-bodied people grow up believing the same thing.

Ordinary life is not made convenient for disabled people – which makes them feel that they can't expect to lead a normal life.

BUT EVERYONE, INCLUDING YOU, HAS THE RIGHT TO BE TREATED FAIRLY.

Disabled people are perfectly able to carry out their own campaigns. If you are disabled in any way, you know that already. If you're not disabled, then your support and energy will be very welcome. Find out from disabled people in your area what problems they encounter, and how you can help. These are some of the questions that will need answering:

- Does the local public transport provide for disabled people?
- How easy is it for disabled people in your area to go to the cinema, or theatre?
- What problems do disabled people find when going to local shops?
- Are there decent public conveniences for disabled people in your area?
- Can disabled people use your school buildings? Is it possible for disabled people to study, teach or work in your school?
- What could be done to improve the facilities for disabled people in your school?
- How can disabled people organise themselves in your area in order to campaign for better facilities?
- How can able-bodied people help to improve facilities for disabled people in your area?

A successful campaign should aim to:

1   find out the facts about facilities for disabled people in your area, and in your school;

2   publicise some of the problems faced by disabled people which could be quickly improved;

3   persuade people in charge to improve facilities – either in school, or in the locality.

Using English to change the world

If you have worked through this Project, you will already have tried out several ways of using English in campaigns.

Choose the campaign that interests you most, and work with a few others who are also interested.

- Find out the facts, and keep a careful record of everything you find out. Write at least one letter asking for further information, and one letter that could be sent to someone influential, asking them to improve things – but only *send* that letter if you want to carry out an actual campaign.
- Design one poster, and produce one leaflet. You could also present a slide show, make a video or produce a magazine.
- When you've done this, show the rest of the class what you have produced.

Then, if you want to go through with a campaign for real – and only if you will follow it through – you can actually launch your campaign on the real world.

You might not feel like changing the world right now. That's fair enough – most of us don't go round saving the world, most of the time.

But at least you should know that you have the right to be involved in serious and important things. And you do need to know how to set about doing things like that if and when you feel like it.

One of the most effective ways of making the world a better place is by using language:

- to find out what's going on;
- to convince people there's a problem;
- to argue for improvement and change.

LANGUAGE IS POWER – USE IT!

Contents

skills sessions

1 How to punctuate speech

Speech punctuation is the way we separate the words spoken by different voices in a story. We use special **speech marks** around all the words that are spoken by characters in the story.

But you could invent your own way of showing when different people are speaking in a story. You could use different colours, underlinings, typefaces – anything you like! – to separate one person talking from another in a story.

Look at how speech is punctuated in this extract from a story:

> Nothing ever got in Emma's way as she cycled to work in the morning, singing along with her personal stereo on her ferrari-red mountain bike. Nothing, that is, except the serious young man who was trying to cross the road that sunny, fateful morning.
> "Watch out!" cried Emma,
> "Watch out yourself," he screamed, as she hurtled into him.
> "I don't believe this," the young man muttered as they fell together in a tangled heap at the side of the road.
> For a moment, neither moved or spoke. Then Emma leapt to her feet, and started dragging her bike from under him.
> "Are you crazy?" he groaned.
> "That's my bike you're lying on," she said, "and I'm in a hurry."

> **1** Write the extract out again, *without* the normal speech punctuation.
> Invent your own way of showing when different people are speaking in the story – by using different colours, underlinings, or lettering.

Speech punctuation is what people normally use to show the reader that the voices in a story are different. There certainly isn't only one perfect way of doing it – what you need to know is how it is usually done in English writing.

> **2** Carry on the story about 'Emma and the young man' for another half-page.
> Punctuate speech the way that it has been done in the extract.

Use this checklist for punctuating English speech when doing this exercise, and check it whenever you want to make sure about how to use speech punctuation:

- Use speech marks at the beginning and end of whatever the characters say.
- Start a new line every time the voice changes.
- Indent each time the voice changes.
- You normally use a comma before phrases like *she said*, *he groaned*.
- Follow *she said*, *he groaned* phrases with a full stop if a new sentence begins immediately after.
- Treat question marks (?) and exclamation marks (!) as if they were commas before *she said*, *he groaned* phrases. In other words, they are not followed by a capital letter.

2 Language commands

Be a word processor

Word processors are computers that help people with the whole business of writing. Like calculators, word processors do whatever they're asked to do – whatever they're programmed to do – in the simplest, most logical way possible. They can:

- store what you write in their memories;
- move bits of writing around;
- edit out parts of your writing that you don't like;
- correct your spelling mistakes;
- check punctuation in your writing;
- find particular kinds of words;
- present your writing in attractive ways.

On a few occasions in this book, you're going to get the chance to be word processors, so that you can learn to do some important and tricky jobs with language in simple and

straightforward ways. Whenever you see the symbol for *language command*, you're

going to act like a word processor. You'll know that you just have to look at the information you're given, and follow the instructions step by step.

Language command – find and count all definite and indefinite articles

You use **definite** and **indefinite articles** all the time, every day. They are the simplest words of all:

definite article = *the*
indefinite articles = *a, an, some*

> 1   Count all the definite articles in the following passage.
> 2   Count all the indefinite articles in the following passage.

In the end, they found the rabbit hiding under a chair in the kitchen. It had seen some birds in the garden, and had panicked when they started singing. It was the most nervous rabbit that had ever lived. When it was just a baby, it had caught sight of its reflection in the kitchen door, and covered almost the whole length of the garden in one terrified leap. It was an albino rabbit, but the man in the shop said that had nothing to do with it – 'some animals are just born stupid,' he said, and pointed to a couple of gormless guinea pigs in the cage behind, to prove the point. Of all the animals they had ever had – and that included a cross-eyed budgerigar, a miserable gerbil and some goldfish – this one really took the biscuit.

3 Roots

Latin and ancient Greek are *dead* languages. No one uses them any more for everyday communication. But the influence of these two dead languages on English is very great. Approximately 50 per cent of the words in English are *based* on Greek and Latin words. For example:

The word *autobiography* is based on three Greek words:
autos = meaning self or same
bios = meaning life
graphein = meaning to write
The word in English is not autosbiosgraphein – autobiography is formed from the **roots** of the three Greek words – auto/bio/graph/.

Look at the family word tree below which shows five words that have grown from the Greek root *auto*.

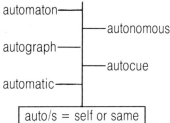

(Use a dictionary to check the meanings of any of the words that are new to you.)

1 Draw a family word tree showing at least five words that have grown from the Greek root *bio* – meaning life.

2 *Graphic* comes from the Greek root graph. Many words in English have grown from *graph*, but they are not so easy to trace because the English word does not begin with the root. Write down any words that you know that have grown from *graph*.

Below are two lists of common Greek and Latin roots. The roots on the left are **prefixes**; a prefix comes at the *beginning* of a word. The roots on the right are **suffixes**; a suffix *ends* a word.

sub –	= under, below (Latin)	– gon	= angle (Greek)
multi –	= many (Latin)	– iatrics	
mal(e) –	= bad, evil (Latin)	– iatry	} = medicine (Greek)
ben(e) –	= good, well (Latin)	– itis	= inflammation (Greek)
mega –	= great (Greek)	– logy	= science of or list (Greek)
micro –	= small (Greek)	– cide	= kill (Latin)
psych(o) –	= mind, soul, spirit (Greek)	– vorous	= eating (Latin)
poly –	= many (Greek)	– rrhea	= flow (Greek)
tele –	= distant, far off (Greek)	– plasm	= matter (Greek)

3 In pairs or small groups, jot down as many words as you can that come from these Greek and Latin roots. Allow yourself 15 minutes.

4 Nouns and adjectives

Nouns

Nouns are *things*. Every noun is something or other. A noun can be a solid thing – something you can touch and see, like a *house* – or a noun can be an invisible thing – something you can talk about or feel, like *sadness*. You can tell if something is a noun by simply saying: *'What thing is this?'*

and by answering: *'a/an . . . '*
                            'the . . . '

If it fits into that kind of question and answer, then it's a noun.

 ## Language command – find and write down all nouns

Look at each of the words, one-by-one, in the following sentence:

I once knew a weird kid who wanted to be a teacher.

question: What thing is this?

answer: a *I*	✗		answer: a *who*	✗
answer: a *once*	✗		answer: a *wanted*	✗
answer: a *knew*	✗		answer: a *to*	✗
answer: a *a*	✗		answer: a *be*	✗
answer: a *weird*	✗		answer: a *a*	✗
answer: a *kid*	✓ (makes sense)		answer: a *teacher*	✓ (makes sense)

So in this sentence, *kid* and *teacher* are nouns.

---

1 Look at each word in the passage below (you have already done the first sentence).

2 Ask the question: *What thing is this?*

3 Answer by saying the word after an indefinite or definite article – in other words:
  a/an . . .
  the . . .

4 If the phrase you say doesn't make sense, it probably isn't a noun. If it sounds all right, it probably is a noun.

5 Write down all the nouns you can find.

I once knew a weird kid who wanted to be a teacher. She spent all her spare time at home trying to get her brother to write essays, or do a scientific experiment, or use a calculator. If he refused, she'd put him in detention, and when Dad came home he'd find the poor little brother sitting in the shed trying to copy out long chunks from a dictionary. He was only six, and he didn't like it much, but his strict sister didn't care, and he knew what would happen to him if he didn't do what he was told.

Adjectives

Adjectives tell you what *kind* of thing something is. Once you've found out how to recognise nouns, it's easy to recognise adjectives. If you find a word that describes what kind of thing a noun is, then it's an adjective. If you find a noun like *house*, and a word which tells you what kind of house it is – like *old* – then that's an adjective.

If it answers the question, *What kind of thing is this noun?* then it's an adjective.

Language command – find and write down all adjectives

Look at each of the words, one-by-one, in this first sentence again:

I once knew a weird kid who wanted to be a teacher.

You know that there are two nouns in this sentence – *kid* and *teacher.* There's nothing to tell you what kind of teacher in that sentence, but there is something that tells you what kind of *kid* – she was a *weird* kid.

question: What kind of thing is this noun (*kid*)?
answer: *weird*

Once you know how to pick out nouns, it's simple to pick out adjectives as well.

> **1** Look at each noun in the following passage.
> **2** See if there are any words that describe what kind of thing each noun is. If that word answers the question *What kind of thing is this noun?* then that word is an adjective.
> **3** Write down all the adjectives you have picked out.

I once knew a weird kid who wanted to be a teacher. She spent all her spare time at home trying to get her brother to write essays, or do a scientific experiment, or use a calculator. If he refused, she'd put him in detention, and when Dad came home he'd find the poor little brother sitting in the shed trying to copy out long chunks from a dictionary. He was only six, and he didn't like it much, but his strict sister didn't care, and he knew what would happen to him if he didn't do what he was told.

> **4** Now take a piece of your own writing, and try to pick out all the nouns and adjectives in that. The more you practise it, the quicker you'll get at it.

5 Punctuation

Punctuation keeps your writing under control

When you write, you choose words. You put them down on paper. You write them clearly enough for people to read them. And you can control *the way* people read them. You can use the following to do this:

commas,   keeping small groups of words under control within sentences

full stops.   the major control device of writing – no sentence is complete without one.

exclamation marks!   when you're trying to make a joke, or to be dramatic

question marks?   whenever you write a question

– dashes –   when you want your writing to move more rapidly

(brackets)   when you need to stick extra information or points into a sentence

paragraphs   each new paragraph means another step forward in what you're writing

colon: especially before lists of points, ideas or information

semi-colons;   especially for separating the points, ideas or information in the list following a colon

underlinings   for emphasis

CAPITAL LETTERS   for greater emphasis, and at the start of sentences

The normal word for these is **punctuation**. You lose control of your words without them: like a car without brakes, accelerator, steering wheel, horn, or indicators. Punctuation keeps your writing under control:

■ it helps steer your writing in the direction you want;
■ it helps to slow it down and speed it up;
■ it helps to indicate what you mean and warn the reader about what's coming.

Proof-read your writing for punctuation

You already use punctuation in your writing – you've heard about full stops, commas, question marks and capital letters before. This Skills Session is about how you can **proof-read** your writing in order to make sure it's under control – to make sure you're using punctuation as cleverly as possible in order to make people read your writing the way you want them to.

The following passage needs to be proof-read in order to check the punctuation:

Oh yes I know what it's like to lose control I remember once when I was about eleven years old it was raining hard the sky was dark it was early November and I had no lights on my bike that was the least of my problems I had been to the cinema I think it was a long time ago so I can't be sure about details I can't remember what the film was for instance anyway it was late afternoon when I came out of the cinema and jumped on my bike knowing that I should have been home two hours ago I pedalled off furiously and despite the rain I was enjoying the ride I used to dream all sorts of dreams on my bike motorcyclist cowboy pilot daredevil hero after a minute or two I was thundering along towards the junction with the main road which was full of traffic at that time of day I was grinning crazily lost in some fantasy of high speed brilliance when I casually pulled at the brake levers only to discover that they didn't work in the rain the bike didn't slow down at all the main road was coming up fast and I just had time to understand that I had the choice between dying under a bus or falling off before I flew in front of the traffic I chose to fall off

Without punctuation, this piece of writing is rushed, out of control, and exhausting to read. The writer has left it to the readers to make whatever sense they can of it. It's the writer's job to help people make sense of their writing.

 ## Language command – apply punctuation

1   Write this passage out, widely spaced and preferably in pencil, so that it is easy to correct. Even better, if you have the opportunity, type it out on a word processor. Apply punctuation – full stops, commas, brackets, colons, semi-colons, and new paragraphs – that *slows down* the writing, that gets it under control.

2   Proof-read the passage a second time, in preparation for changing the way you have just punctuated and controlled it in as many ways as necessary in order to *speed up* the writing, and make it more dramatic.
    If you think about it, this particular passage is about going fast and being out of control, so why not use punctuation that helps to create that feeling for the reader? There's no need to write it out again. Simply get rid of any of the punctuation you put in before that slows down the writing too much and, instead, put in punctuation such as exclamation marks, underlinings, CAPITALS, and dashes if they help to create the effect you're after.

6 How to write tabloid news stories

The first thing to decide when you write a tabloid news story is: What is the *one* thing I am going to tell people about this story? A good tabloid story usually makes a big deal out of just ONE thing that has happened. You can use the skills of tabloid journalism to make a **big deal!** out of any story you choose.

Headlines!

Tabloid headlines usually tell you what the story is about, very briefly. They are usually written as simple phrases like the one opposite:

JOHN'S HYENA LAUGH GETS HIM BANNED BY CLUB

A good tabloid headline squeezes as much **drama** as it can from the story it tells.

Paragraphs

Tabloid stories are made up of several short **paragraphs**. Each paragraph in a tabloid story usually consists of just ONE sentence.

The opening words of the *first* paragraph of tabloid stories often begin by naming the main person in the story, and by saying what *type* of person this is:

Merry miner John Hill   Blushing bridegroom Mike Stonehouse
Superman pilot Bill Parks   Dazzling Princess Di   Gallant Prince Andrew
Hell-raising actor Brian Watkins   Olympic hero Nigel Fish

The rest of the first paragraph then goes on to tell you the *main point* of the story again, but in a bit more detail than the headline:

Merry miner John Hill has been banned from his local club – because his "hyena laugh" drove drinkers up the wall.

The other paragraphs gradually fill in the background details to the story:

■ who else was involved;
■ where it happened;
■ how old the people involved were.

There is usually at least one paragraph where one of the people involved is quoted – where they say something about what happened:

The secretary confirmed: "John's behaviour has upset . . . members"

All these details are considered necessary in newspaper stories. The idea is that readers will only take the story seriously if it is full of *facts* – like names, ages and places.

If there are several paragraphs, *mini-headlines* are used to spread out the story, and keep up the readers' interest.

JOHN'S HYENA LAUGH GETS HIM BANNED BY CLUB

He put other members off darts and dominoes

By JOHN SCOTT

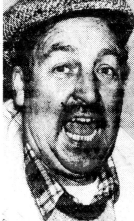

MERRY miner John Hill has been banned from his local club—because his "hyena laugh" drove drinkers up the wall.

Barmen refused to serve 50-year-old John after the committee summoned him to a "kangaroo court"—and he didn't turn up.

But John, from Cannock, Staffs, wasn't joking yesterday when he said: "I'm very upset and I won't be going back. The club was too quiet for me anyway—they're a bunch of wallabies down there.

"I didn't go to meet the committee because their letter made it sound like a kangaroo court."

The secretary of Broomhill Albion Working Men's Club, Syd Bailey, confirmed: "John's behaviour has upset a number of members.

"We wanted to tell him to calm down a bit."

Another club regular explained: "John is a great bloke, but his laughing gets on everyone's nerves.

Confessed

"People here take their games of darts, dominoes and cards seriously and he ruins their concentration.

"*He sits down and suddenly starts laughing hysterically for no apparent reason. He is like a hyena.*"

John confessed last night: "I make a joke out of almost anything and like a good laugh.

"But it is not funny having people make a personal complaint like that about you.

"From now on I'll be going somewhere else for a drink."

He added: "I've never had any complaints from my wife Margaret.

"We've rowed about lots of things, but never that."

John . . . loony laugh

Language

If you look carefully at tabloids, you'll notice that certain words are used all the time. Words like:

probed   ordeal   clashed   plucky   outrage   tragic   shock   riddle

All of these words are used to make the story as dramatic as possible.

> **1** Look through a collection of tabloid papers, and see what words you can find, that often appear in news stories. Look for the typical kinds of words that are used to make stories seem as dramatic as possible. Decide what they really mean. Make as big a list of words like these as you can, and use them for the next activity.
>
> **2** Now write your own tabloid news story about something very ordinary and undramatic. Use as many of the methods described here to write the story:
> - as clearly and readably as possible,
> - as dramatically as possible.

You could write about:

- someone spilling their cornflakes at breakfast;
- a budgy escaping from its cage and getting stuck in the larder;
- an announcement made in school assembly by the deputy head, saying that light blue jumpers may now be worn by pupils in the third form and above.

7 Controlling readers' expectations

1 Read the following two openings to stories. What might happen in each story? How has the story been set up in these opening lines? What are the readers meant to *expect*?

■ Andy had felt uneasy, right from the moment he woke up that day. It was as if something
was going to happen today, but he didn't know what it was. He sat in the kitchen, stroking his faithful old dog Ned, and tried to tell himself there was nothing to worry about.
'You're my best friend, Ned,' he murmured, to the poor, near-blind old animal. 'I don't know what I'd do without you.'
His mother called him from upstairs, and asked him to bring the vacuum cleaner up to her. He patted Ned on the head, and opened the kitchen door for him in case he wanted to go out. Then he hurried off to find the vacuum cleaner.

■ Suzie slammed the front door behind her, and strode off up the street without turning to look back even once. She was finished, she could never forgive him. She was so angry,
she hardly noticed the pouring rain that drenched her clothes and ran down her face, mingling with her bitter tears.
Minutes later she was on the dual carriageway, leaving that town, his town, for ever. Never coming back. It was nearly midnight, and the headlights of the occasional car passing by on the other side were dazzling through the wet windscreen. Suzie gritted her teeth and pushed the throttle of her fragile little Mini to the floor. She just wanted to get away from that town, and never come back. She gripped the wheel and stared wildly through the wild weather at the road ahead, as she thundered through the night, still sobbing uncontrollably.

In the two extracts above, both stories begin by setting up certain kinds of expectations: as soon as you start reading them, you begin to think about *what might happen*. You wonder about things like:

■ Will the dog get hurt? Will the boy be sad? Is something terrible going to happen?
■ Will Suzie have an accident? Will she be all right? Will she make up with her boyfriend?

Different people might not expect exactly the same things, but they'll probably all expect the same *sorts* of things.

Think of the way you get warned about things that are going to happen in films. If you're allowed to catch sight of a gun at the start of a film, you can be sure that someone's going to be shot by the end.

In any story, everything that you are told, or shown, is there for a purpose. Everything you're told or shown in a story helps to set up your expectations about what might happen in the story.

The whole point of a good story is to take the readers for a ride, a sort of magical mystery tour – keep the readers wondering what's going to happen, and looking for clues to tell them where they're going.

2　Write an opening half-page of a story called *ACCIDENT!*

The beginning of this particular story can be about someone who is going to end up sooner or later having to be taken to the emergency ward in a hospital. Because of the title, anyone who reads this story will already be expecting something to go wrong. **Story titles** are a very effective way of making people expect certain things to happen in a story.

When you write your opening paragraphs for this story, try to do the following things:

■ take your time – build up the readers' expectations slowly;
■ drop hints and clues about what might happen, and how it might happen;
■ you might want to get them worried about one thing, and then shock them with something unexpected.

Your job, when you write the opening for this story, is to get the readers looking for *clues* in the opening paragraphs about what is going to happen. There wouldn't be much suspense in a story that goes like this:

> Jack Smith fell off a ladder while cleaning some upstairs windows and banged his head, so he was taken to a casualty ward where he nearly died and then he got better. The End.

Set up any accident you like – you can choose the one about falling off a ladder if you want. Don't get as far as describing the accident. Just set up some worries (clues) in the readers' minds about what might go wrong.

3　Write the opening half-page of a story called *DISAPPOINTMENT.*

The title will immediately get the readers ready for what might happen. Now give them some good clues to get them guessing.

4　Swop your story openings with a partner, and write the next bit of your partner's story, without discussing what the person who wrote the opening had in mind.

■ Figure out what the opening to the story has made you expect.
■ Decide what will actually happen, and whether it will be different from what you've been led to expect.
■ Make it happen.

8 How to use a thesaurus

Read this first draft of the opening of a story written for younger children.

> Nathan was very excited. He grabbed his coat, shouted 'goodbye' to his grandmother, and ran off down the road. He ran as fast as he could and, for once, he didn't even bother to jump over the cracks in the pavement.
>
> He ran past the bus stop, and kept on running until he came to the centre of town. His legs were getting tired and he was out of breath and he began running more slowly.
>
> There were people everywhere. To his surprise, they were all running too. Some were running slowly while others looked like real athletes and were running very quickly . . .

The writer is running out of words. She wants to give her readers a picture of Nathan running along and finding himself in the middle of a marathon, but she can't think of the words to use. It's at this point that a **thesaurus** would prove really useful.

A thesaurus (it comes from the Greek word meaning 'treasure') is a *reference book* that puts words into *groups*. Each group contains words that are similar in meaning to each other or are related to each other because they are about the same topic or subject.

Look at the sample pages of a thesaurus printed opposite.

■ To find other words to use instead of *run*, you would first look at the back of the thesaurus (in this example, page 1097). There you will see all the different sections you could refer to, to find words similar in meaning.

■ You decide to look at *move fast* 277. This will be section 277 (in this example, on page 163). All the sections with words of similar meaning are at the beginning of the thesaurus.

> **1** Use the words you have found to improve the story above. First write down any words that you think the writer of the story about Nathan could consider using. Then use these words to redraft the story.

Read this note from a postcard written by someone who's really stuck for words.

> Having a nice time! The hotel's nice and the food's nice too. So far the weather's been nice and not too hot. The local people are very nice and we've been to some really nice places.

> **2** Look up the word *nice* in your thesaurus, and follow up any cross-references. Select the words that you think could be used, and then re-write the postcard avoiding the word nice.

1097

runlet

rulership
position of authority
733 n.
rules and regulations
practice 610 n.
right 913 n.
rules of business
conduct 688 n.
ruling
judgment 480 n.
legal trial 959 n.
ruling class
authority 733 n.
master 741 n.
upper class 868 n.
ruling passion
eccentricity 503 n.
opinionatedness
602 n.
affections 817 n.
rum
unusual 84 adj.
alcoholic drink
301 n.
ridiculous 849 adj.
rumba
dance 837 n.
rumble
roll 403 vb.
understand 516 vb.
fight 716 n.
rumbustious
disorderly 61 adj.
loud 400 adj.
riotous 738 adj.
excitable 822 adj.
ruminant
animal 365 n.adj.
ruminate
graze 301 vb.
meditate 449 vb.
ruminative
thoughtful 449 adj.
rummage
search 459 vb.
rummer
cup 194 n.
rummy
card game 837 n.
rumour
insubstantial thing
4 n.
topic 452 n.
publication 528 n.
rumour 529 n.vb.
fable 543 n.
rump
remainder 41 n.
buttocks 238 n.
rumple
jumble 63 vb.
roughen 259 vb.
fold 261 n.vb.
agitate 318 vb.
rumpus
turmoil 61 n.
violence 176 n.
quarrel 709 n.
fight 716 n.

run
separate 46 vb.
come unstuck 49 vb.
continuity 71 n.
series 71 n.
discontinuity 72 n.
generality 79 n.
recurrence 106 n.
elapse 111 vb.
continuance 146 n.
motion 265 n.
pedestrianism 267 n.
voyage 269 vb.
move fast 277 vb.
following 284 n.
flow out 298 vb.
liquefy 337 vb.
flow 350 vb.
lose colour 426 vb.
edition 589 n.
habit 610 n.
chase 619 n.
run away 620 vb.
be active 678 vb.
hasten 680 vb.
deal with 688 vb.
manage 689 vb.
steal 788 vb.
amuse oneself
837 vb.
— after
pursue 619 vb.
desire 859 vb.
court 889 vb.
— amok
be violent 176 vb.
go mad 503 vb.
be excitable 822 vb.
— at
attack 712 vb.
charge 712 vb.
— a temperature
be hot 379 vb.
— away
move fast 277 vb.
decamp 296 vb.
run away 620 vb.
seek safety 660 vb.
escape 667 vb.
— away with
take away 786 vb.
— away with an idea
be credulous 487 vb.
— counter (to)
be contrary 14 vb.
counteract 182 vb.
tell against 467 vb.
— down
decrease 37 vb.
cease 145 vb.
collide 279 vb.
underestimate
483 vb.
pursue 619 vb.
make insufficient
636 vb.
charge 712 vb.
be malevolent
898 vb.

not respect 921 vb.
dispraise 924 vb.
detract 926 vb.
— for
steer for 281 vb.
offer oneself 759 vb.

— through
make uniform
16 vb.
consume 165 vb.
prevail 178 vb.
pervade 189 vb.

276-277 Space

163

booster; nose cone, warhead; guided missile, intercontinental ballistic m. 723 *missile weapon*; doodlebug, V1, V2.

spaceship, spacecraft, space probe, space capsule, space shuttle; lunar module; space station, sputnik 321 *satellite*; flying saucer, UFO, unidentified flying object.

Adj. *aviational*, aeronautical, aerospace; aerodynamic, aerostatic; astronautical, space-travelling; airworthy 271 *flying*; heavier-than-air, lighter-than-air; supersonic; vertical take-off.

See: 1, 2, 269, **271**, 275, 300, 321, **722**, **723.** .

277 Velocity

N. *velocity*, celerity, rapidity, speed, swiftness, fleetness, quickness, liveliness, alacrity, agility; instantaneousness, speed of thought 116 *instantaneity*; no loss of time, promptness, expedition, dispatch; speed, tempo, rate, pace, bat 265 *motion*; speed-rate, miles per hour, knots; Mach number; speed of light, speed of sound, supersonic speed; great speed, lightning s.; maximum speed, express s., full s., full steam; utmost speed, press of sail, full s.; precipitation, hurry, flurry 680 *haste*; reckless speed, breakneck s. 857 *rashness*; streak, blue s., streak of lightning, flash, lightning f.; flight, jet f., supersonic f.; gale, hurricane, tempest, torrent; electricity, telegraph, lightning, greased l.; speed measurement, tachometer, speedometer 465 *gauge*; wind gauge 340 *pneumatics*; log, logline; speed trap 542 *trap*.

spurt, acceleration, speed-up, overtaking; burst, burst of speed, burst of energy; thrust, drive, impetus 279 *impulse*; jump, spring, bound, pounce 312 *leap*; whiz, swoop, swoosh, zip, uprush, zoom; down rush, dive, power d.; flying start, rush, dash, scamper, run, sprint, gallop, tantivy.

speeding, driving, hard d., scorching, racing, burn-up; bowling along, rattling a., batting a.; course, race, career, full c.; full speed, full lick; pace, smart p., rattling p., spanking rate, fair clip; quick march, double, forced march 680 *haste*; clean pair of heels, quick retreat 667 *escape*; race course, speed track 716 *racing*.

speeder, hustler, speed merchant, speed maniac, scorcher, racing driver 268 *driver*; runner, harrier; racer, sprinter; galloper; courser, racehorse 273 *thorough*-

bred; greyhound, cheetah, hare, deer, doe, gazelle, antelope; ostrich, eagle, swallow; arrow, arrow from the bow, bullet, cannonball 287 *missile*; jet, rocket; speedboat, clipper 275 *ship*; express, express train; express messenger, Ariel, Mercury 529 *courier*; magic carpet, seven-league boots.

Adj. *speedy*, swift, fast, quick, rapid, nimble, volant; darting, dashing, lively, brisk, smart, snappy, nifty, zippy 174 *vigorous*; wasting no time, expeditious, hustling 680 *hasty*; double-quick, rapid-fire; prompt 135 *early*; immediate 116 *instantaneous*; high-geared, high-speed, adapted for speed, streamlined, souped-up; speeding, racing, ton-up; running, charging, runaway; flying, whizzing, hurtling, pelting; whirling, tempestuous; breakneck, headlong, precipitate 857 *rash*; fleet, fleet of foot, wing-footed, light-f., nimble-f., quick-f.; darting, starting, flashing; swift-moving, agile, nimble, slippery, evasive; mercurial, like quicksilver 152 *changeful*; winged, eagle-w., like a bird; arrowy, like an arrow; like a flash, like greased lightning, like the wind, quick as lightning, quick as thought, quick as the wind, like a bat out of hell; meteoric, electric, telegraphic, transonic, supersonic, hypersonic, jet-propelled.

Vb. *move fast*, move, shift, travel, speed; drive, pelt, streak, flash, shoot; scorch, burn up the miles, scour the plain, tear up the road; scud, career; skim, nip, cut; bowl along 258 *go smoothly*; sweep along, tear a., rattle a., thunder a., storm a.; tear, rip, zip, rush, dash; fly, wing, whiz, skirr; hurtle, zoom, dive; dash off, tear o., dart o., dash on, dash forward; plunge, lunge, swoop; run, trot, double, lope, spank, gallop; bolt, cut and run, hotfoot it, leg it, scoot, skedaddle, scamper, scurry, skelter, scuttle; show a clean pair of heels 620 *run away*; hare, run like a h., run like the wind, run like mad, run like the clappers; start, dart, dartle, flit; frisk, whisk; spring, bound, leap, jump, pounce; ride hard, put one's best foot forward, stir one's stumps, get cracking, get a move on; hie, hurry, post, haste 680 *hasten*; chase, charge, stampede, career, go full tilt, go full pelt, go full lick, go full bat, go full steam, go all out; break the speed limit, break the sound barrier.

accelerate, speed up, raise the tempo; gather

9 How to use a dictionary

A **dictionary** is a reference book that lists the words in a language in alphabetical order. It gives the user information about the spelling, pronunciation, meaning, history and use of words. A dictionary gives a picture of the language as it is used at a given time. English is growing and developing all the time, so new dictionaries are published and existing dictionaries are revised and changed to reflect the changes in the language. It is important for you to use a dictionary that is up-to-date.

The words in a dictionary are arranged in alphabetical order. It's obvious that the word *yoghurt* comes after *apple*. Many words, however, begin with the same letter or letters, and to find the **alphabetical order**, you have to go further and further into each word.

> 1   Arrange the following words in alphabetical order:
>   cello   catastrophe   careless   cat   cellophane   carnival   cautious
>   cauliflower   category   card

Look at the sample dictionary page shown opposite. Notice that there are two words in heavy type at the top of the page. These are **guide words**. They tell you whether the word you're looking for is on a particular page.

The first word on the page is *carving*, and the final one is *catcall*. If, for example, you're looking for the word *cassette* you know that you've found the right page because cassette comes alphabetically between these two words.

Here are some other pairs of guide words taken from the dictionary.

    call off   cancel (page 45)
    cancellation   capstan (page 46)
    capsule   career (page 47)
    career   carve (page 48)

> 2   On which page would you find each of the following words?
>   caravan   caricature   canoe   calypso   canyon   campaign

Get hold of the dictionary you regularly use in school and read the **introductory pages** in which the layout of the book, and the symbols and abbreviations used in it are explained to you. To make the most of your dictionary, you need to understand how it works.

> 3   Jot down answers to the following questions. Use your dictionary to help you.
>   What is an immersion heater?
>   What language does the word *myth* come from?
>   What are the different meanings of *pass* when used as a verb?
>   What does a *lexicographer* do?

carving · 49 · **catcall**

or stone) in order to make a special, usu. decorative, shape **2** to cut (cooked meat) into pieces or slices **3** to make or get by hard work: *He carved out a name for himself* — **∼r** *n*

carving *n* something shaped or made by carving

caryatid *n technical* a pillar shaped like a clothed female figure

cascade¹ *n* anything that seems to pour or flow downward

cascade² *v* **-caded, -cading** to pour in quantity

case¹ *n* **1** an example: *a case of stupidity* **2** a particular occasion or state of affairs: *Pauline's stupid, but it's different in the case of Mary; she's just lazy* **3 a** (of diseases) a single example: *This is a case of fever* **b** a person suffering from an illness **4 a** a set of events needing police inquiry **b** a person being dealt with by the police, a social worker, etc. **5** a question to be decided in a court of law **6** the facts and arguments supporting one side in a disagreement or in a question brought before a court: *The police have a clear case against the prisoner* **7** (in grammar) (changes in) the form of a word (esp. of a noun, adjective, or pronoun) showing its relationship with other words in a sentence **8 in case** for fear that; lest; because it may happen that **9 in case of a** for fear that (that stated event) should happen: *We insured the house in case of fire* **b** if (the stated event) should happen: *Break the glass in case of fire*

case² *n* **1** a container in which goods can be stored or moved **2** a suitcase **3** an outer covering for holding a filling: *a pastry case*

case³ *v* **cased, casing** to enclose or cover with a case

casein *n* a protein found in milk and cheese —**caseous** *adj*

case law *n* law which is established by an earlier judgement (PRECEDENT) rather than by legislation —see illustration at LEGISLATION

casement window also **casement**— *n* a window that opens like a door —compare SASH WINDOW

case study *n* a thorough study of something (e g a person, organization or situation) as a way of finding out more about things of that kind

casework *n* social work concerned with the difficulties of a particular person, family, etc. — **∼er** *n*

cash¹ *n* money in coins and notes

cash² *v* to exchange (a cheque or other order to pay) for cash

cash and carry *n, adj* (a usu. large shop where goods are) sold cheaply if paid for at once and taken away by the buyer

cash crop *n* a crop produced for sale, not for the grower's use —compare SUBSISTENCE CROP

cash desk *n* (in a shop) the desk where payments are made

cashew *n* a type of tropical American tree or its small curved nut

cash flow *n* the flow of money payments to, from, or within a business

cashier *n* a person in charge of money receipts and payments in a bank, hotel, shop, etc.

cash in *v adv* to take advantage or profit (from): *Let's cash in on the fine weather and go out for the day*

cashmere *n* fine soft wool from a type of goat which lives in Kashmir

cash on delivery *n* payment to be made at the time and place of delivery

cash register *n* a machine in shops for calculating and recording the amount of each sale and the money received

casing *n* **1** a protective covering, esp. the

outer rubber covering of a car tyre **2** the frame of a door or window

casino *n* **-nos 1** a building used for gambling **2** a type of card game for two or four players

cask *n* a barrel-shaped container for holding liquids

casket *n* an ornamental box for holding small valuable things

casserole *n* a deep covered dish in which food may be cooked and served

cassette *n* **1** a container for photographic film which can be fitted into a camera **2** a container holding magnetic tape which can be fitted into a cassette recorder —see illustration at DATA

cassette recorder *n* an apparatus which can make and play back recordings on cassette

cassock *n* a long garment worn by priests and by people helping at religious services

cast¹ *v* **cast, casting 1** to throw or drop **2** to throw off; remove: *Every year the snake casts (off) its skin* **3** to give (a vote) **4** to give an acting part to (a person) **5** to make (an object) by pouring hot metal (or plastic) into a mould **6** to make and put into effect (a spell)

cast² *n* **1** an act of throwing **2** the actors in a play, moving picture, etc. **3** a stiff protective covering of cloth and cement, for holding a broken bone in place while it gets better — see also PLASTER CAST **4** general shape or quality: *the noble cast of his head* **5** *becoming rare* a slight squint **6** a small pile of earth left by worms when they make a hole

castanets *n* a musical instrument made from two shells of hard wood fastened to the thumb by a string and played by being knocked together by the fingers

castaway *n* **-ways 1** a person surviving shipwreck by reaching the shore of a strange country **2** a person made to leave a ship by force and left on land

cast away *v adv* to leave (someone) somewhere as the result of a shipwreck

cast down *v adv* to lower in spirit; upset

caste *n* **1** division of society based on differences of wealth, rank, rights, profession, or job **2** any of the groups resulting from this division, in which a person usu. finds himself at birth, esp. one of the social classes of Hindu society

castellated *adj technical* (of a building) having defences like a castle

caster, -or *n* **1** a small wheel fixed to the base of a piece of furniture so that it can be easily moved **2** a container with small holes in the top so that sugar, salt, etc. may be evenly spread over foods —compare SALTCELLAR

caster sugar *n* very fine white sugar

castigate *v* **-gated, -gating** *esp. written* **1** to punish severely in order to correct **2** to express strong disapproval of (a person, behaviour, or someone's ideas) — **-gation** *n*

casting *n* **1** an object shaped by having been cast **2** the act of choosing actors for a play or film **3** (in fishing) the act of throwing the hook, fastened to the line, into the water

cast-iron *adj* **1** made of cast iron **2** hard; unbreakable; unyielding

cast iron *n* a hard but brittle type of iron, made by pouring molten iron into a mould

castle¹ *n* **1** a strongly-built building made in former times to be defended against attack **2** also **rook**— (in the game of chess) one of the powerful pieces placed on the corner squares of the board at the beginning of each game

castle² *v* **-tled, -tling** (in the game of chess) to move the king two squares towards either of his own castles and put the castle on the square that the king has moved across

cast-off *adj* (esp. of clothes) unwanted by

someone else —**castoff** *n*

cast off *v adv* **1** (of a boat or ship) to set free or be set free on the water by untying a rope **2** to give or throw away (clothes no longer wanted) **3** (in knitting) to remove (stitches) from the needle in such a way that the finished garment does not come undone

cast on *v adv* (in knitting) to put (the first stitches) onto a needle

castor *n* a caster

castor oil *n* a thick fatty oil made from the seeds of the **castor-oil plant** and used esp. as a laxative

castor sugar *n* CASTER SUGAR

castrate *v* **-trated, -trating** to remove the sex organs of (an animal or person) —compare EMASCULATE, NEUTER, SPAY — **-tration** *n*

casual¹ *adj* **1** resulting from chance **2** not serious or thorough **3** informal; not for special use **4** not close: *a casual friendship* **5** (of workers) employed for a short period of time — **∼ly** *adv* — **∼ness** *n*

casual² *n* a person employed for a short period of time

casualty *n* **-ties 1** a person hurt or killed in an accident or war **2** a person or thing defeated or destroyed **3** also **casualty ward, department**— a place in a hospital where people hurt in accidents are treated

cat *n* **1** a small animal with soft fur and sharp teeth and claws, often kept as a pet or in buildings to catch mice and rats **2** any of various types of animals related to this, such as the lion or tiger **3 let the cat out of the bag** *esp. spoken* to tell a secret (often unintentionally) **4 rain cats and dogs** *esp. spoken* to rain very heavily

catabolism *n* the chemical process in living things which breaks down complicated substances into simple ones, often releasing energy —**catabolic** *adj*

cataclysm *n* a violent and sudden change or event, esp. a serious flood or earthquake — **-mic** *adj*

catacomb *n* an underground burial place with many passages and rooms △ HECATOMB

catalase *n* an enzyme found in plant and animal tissues, that breaks down hydrogen peroxide into oxygen and water

catalogue *n, v* **-logued, -loguing** (to make) a list of places, names, goods, etc. in a special order so that they can be found easily

catalyst *n* **1** a substance which, without itself changing, causes chemical activity to quicken **2** a person or thing that causes or speeds up change — **-lytic** *adj* — **-lysis** *n*

catalytic converter *n* a device in a motor vehicle, that uses catalysts to reduce the poisonous and polluting substances in exhaust fumes

catamaran *n* a type of boat with two narrow parallel hulls

cat-and-mouse *adj esp. spoken* consisting of continuous chasing, near-seizures and waiting for the right moment to attack

catapult *n, v* **1** (to use) a small Y-shaped stick with a rubber band fastened between the forks to shoot small stones at objects **2** (to use) a powerful apparatus for helping planes take off from a ship —compare ARRESTER WIRES **3** (to use) a machine for throwing heavy stones into the air, used in former times as a weapon for breaking down walls

cataract *n* **1** a large waterfall or steep swiftly flowing stretch of river **2** *medical* a growth on the eye causing a slow loss of sight

catarrh *n* (a disease causing) a flow of thick liquid (MUCUS) in the nose and throat, as when one has a cold — **∼al** *adj*

catastrophe *n* a sudden and terrible event that causes suffering, misfortune, or ruin — **-phic** *adj* — **-phically** *adv*

cat burglar *n* a thief who enters buildings by climbing up walls, pipes, etc.

catcall *v, n* (to make) a loud whistle

10 Impersonal writing (without using I)

Impersonal writing is a way of using language for a particular purpose. Sometimes things are clearer if you *leave yourself out* of something you're writing. It can help you to understand what went on better, if you say nothing about what you did or felt.

Sometimes you are *required* to write like that – in school or at work.

This piece of impersonal writing is a report of an experiment that has been carried out into how to make the best mashed potato. The *only* purpose of this writing is to explain the things that were done to make good mashed potato.

Report on mashed potato experiment

It was discovered that the most delicious mashed potato is made from King Edwards potatoes, using the following method of preparation: first, the King Edwards were peeled and cut into medium-sized pieces (any smaller and they broke up during boiling). The pieces were placed in salted, boiling water and boiled for approximately 18 minutes, until they were soft but firm. They were drained thoroughly, and any remaining moisture was steamed off over a light heat. When powdery and dry, they were mashed up carefully with a potato masher. Plenty of fresh ground pepper and a dash of nutmeg was added, along with 2 tablespoons of thick cream. They were mashed again, more pepper was added, and placed in a bowl. Butter was placed on top, and they were then ready for immediate serving.

Impersonal writing is a skill you can use when you just need to present the facts about something to readers, and when you need to show that you understand exactly what went on in whatever you're describing – for instance, in a scientific experiment. Your own *mood, feelings, mistakes, opinions* can all be left out of this kind of writing. The purpose is to present a cold, factual and sensible description of what the readers need to know – and nothing else. Follow these simple guidelines for impersonal writing:

- In impersonal writing, just concentrate on what the reader needs to know.
- In impersonal writing, mention yourself as little as possible. Try to avoid using words like: I/me/mine/myself. Instead of saying:

  > I peeled and chopped up the King Edwards into pieces that weren't exactly big or small.

  you can say:

  > The King Edwards were peeled and cut into medium-sized pieces.

- In impersonal writing, avoid words that chiefly explain your feelings and opinions. Instead of saying:

  > I let the potatoes go all runny – they looked really disgusting.

  you can say:

  > The potatoes became excessively liquid.

  Avoid words that usually just give your opinion, words like: lovely, horrible, wonderful, disgusting, brilliant, rubbish.

Think of other things that could have gone on during a mashed potato experiment:

You might have cut yourself peeling the potatoes, and burnt yourself cooking them. You might have ended up covered in runny potato, and feeling sick. The teacher might have put the whole class in detention for the mashed potato fight which ended the lesson.

---

1 Write a completely different version of this event. This time, don't use impersonal writing – don't write an experiment report. Write a *poem* about the feelings and sensations you might have experienced during a lesson like this.
Use lots of words that convey the emotions and sensations of peeling, chopping, steaming, mashing, tasting and getting into trouble. When you've finished, underline all the words that would not belong in a piece of impersonal writing.

Impersonal writing is sometimes a way of covering up what went on in a particular event. Read these two versions of the same incident, both written by the same person:

Why I Have Been Treated Unfairly, by Sonia Eagleton form 3G,

I reckon it's completely disgusting that I've been blamed for what happened to that rotten student teacher. It was totally stupid of him to keep just me in over lunch. Just because I threw my tomato sandwich over to my friend, and the student teacher happened to step in the way and get the sandwich in his ugly face. I mean, it wasn't just me who laughed. He looked dead funny, anyway.

Misbehavior Report by Sonia Eagleton form 3G

This is a report of the incident with the student teacher, during which he was struck on the face by a small, soft object. Owing to his moving unexpectedly into the path of a sandwich being delivered to another pupil, the student teacher unfortunately collided with this article. A certain amount of humour was then expressed by the whole class, resulting in the student teacher placing the full blame for the uproar on the original owner of the sandwich, S. Eagleton, who is innocent.

---

2 Write two accounts of an incident like this, where you are trying to argue against getting into trouble:
First write an account which expresses a strong **personal** point of view about what happened – concentrating on *yourself*, on *your own* feelings and opinions about what went on. Read through what you've written and underline all the words that would not belong in a piece of impersonal writing.
Now write an account which hides your feelings and opinions, and which presents a less emotional, more **impersonal** point of view, using the skills of impersonal writing you have learned.

11   Is it clear?

Read the following advice:

> On those occasions when, as a speaker or writer, one wishes to convey information to others (and, in this instance, others should be taken to mean the general public as opposed to experts who may well share the specialist knowledge of the speaker or writer), it is incumbent on one to ensure that all that is said or written is comprehended by one's audience.
>
> Thus, it is of the utmost importance that the vocabulary of any such communication – spoken or written – be judiciously selected: esoteric, archaic, obscure and words of a technical nature should be eschewed whenever possible, as should those open to multiple interpretation. Moreover, complex syntactical structures dependent on an inordinately high number of subordinate clauses, and ones such as will render the speech or writing incomprehensible to all save the cognescenti, should have no place in the aforementioned communications.

Were you annoyed by this piece of writing? Did you understand it? Could you follow the advice? The language in the passage you have just tried to read is complicated, pompous and very difficult to understand. The writer has failed to think about what it would be like to *read* that passage.

1   Read through the passage again, and find at least two examples of each of the following:
  ■ words that most people would not understand;
  ■ long, complicated sentences.

2   Find a passage of writing that is particularly annoying to read because it hasn't been written clearly enough. Look in a school textbook (*this* book, for instance) or an instruction manual. Again, pick out the difficult words and any long complicated sentences that are hard to follow.

3   Write a set of guidelines to help any writer to avoid writing unclearly. Make sure you write your guidelines in plain, clear English that most people would be able to understand. Set out your guidelines in any way you prefer. Number the points you make if you think that will help to make it easier to understand.

4   Re-write the passage, making it as clear as possible. Think about layout and the design of the page, as well as the language.

12 What is a prefix?

Some groups of letters or sounds have no meaning on their own. They only come to life when they are *attached* to another word. For example:

un doesn't mean anything in English, but when you add it to the beginning of a word, it is very powerful. It helps to make a new word that is opposite in meaning.

un– + happy = unhappy
un– + known = unknown

Un– is a **prefix**. A prefix is a group of letters (sometimes a single letter), placed at the beginning of a word to make a new word.

Understanding how prefixes work can help you with your spelling. For example:

knowing that *disappear* is made up of *dis–* + *appear*, you are less likely to write dissappear. Similarly, you are more likely to spell *dissatisfy* correctly when you know that it is made up of *dis–* + *satisfy*.

> **1** Write down the opposite in meaning to each of the following words by adding the prefix *dis–* to the beginning of the word.
>
> ability   advantage   agreement   appearance   armament
> connect   continue   infected   integrate   satisfaction
>
> Check your spelling by looking up the words you have written in a dictionary.

There are other prefixes like *un-* and *dis-* which are so powerful that when added to the beginning of a word they form a new word that is opposite in meaning. For example:

ir– + relevant = irrelevant   in– + expensive = inexpensive
im– + possible = impossible   il– + legal   = illegal

> **2** Allow yourself ten minutes only, and write down as many words as you can think of that are formed in this way with one of the prefixes: *ir–*, *im–*, *in–*, or *il–*.

Understanding that some words are made by a prefix attached to the beginning of a word can also help you to increase your vocabulary and to work out the meanings of words you haven't come across before. For example:

pre–   = before a particular time or event. So *premature* means happening too early.
tri–   = three. A *tricycle* (or trike) has three wheels.
semi– = half or partly. So *semi-skimmed* milk is partly skimmed.
anti– = opposed to, or against something. So the *anti-apartheid* movement
         is an organsation opposed to the system of apartheid in South Africa.

> **3** Write down at least three words that begin with each of the prefixes above: *pre–*, *tri–*, *semi–*, *anti–*, a total of twelve words. Use a dictionary if you need help.

13 Verbs

Nouns, adjectives, adverbs, prepositions, connectives, articles are all *parts* of language, just as wheels, seats, tyres, steering columns, chassis, gear boxes, doors and windows are all *parts* of cars.

The parts of cars need to fit together properly if they're going to be able to work together as a car. Then something is needed to give the car life, to make it go – an engine. The parts of language also need to fit together properly, if they're going to be able to work together as sentences. Then something has got to make them go – a **verb**.

Verbs are the engines of sentences – they make sentences work.

Here is a lifeless list of words, that don't work as a sentence yet. They need a verb to make them work:

Stella   her spaceship safely on the dark planet.

> **1**   Choose a word that brings this set of words to life, that makes it work as a sentence – it's bound to be a *verb*.

Often, sentences use more than one verb:

When Stella   the inhabitants of the planet, she   away.

> **2**   What verbs would turn this list of words into a working sentence?

Sentences don't work until they've got at least *one* verb in them.

There are two types of verb:

■ **main verbs** – such as *talk*, *write*, and *go* – give you most information about what's happening. For example:

Spacewoman Stella *goes* to a new planet every week.

■ **auxiliary verbs** – these support main verbs and tell us more about what's happening, when it's happening, if it ought to happen, if it has to happen. Their job is to help the main verb. For example:

can   could   may   might   shall   should
will   would   must   ought to

Stella *ought to* go home.
Stella *could* go to the moon instead.

These auxiliary verbs can also help sentences to work:

be: am   is   are   was   were   been   being
have: has   have   had   having
do: do   does   did   done   doing

For example: Stella *has* gone to Mars.

Many of these auxiliary verbs often get shortened in speech and writing. We use **apostrophes** to fill in the gaps. For example:

I am gets shortened to *I'm.*
We have gets shortened to *we've.*
Stella has gone to Mars gets shortened to *Stella's gone to Mars.*

Language depends on verbs. They've got an important job to do, and they need to come in many different versions to cope with all that work. All the different versions of verbs can help you to say or write what you want to.

3   Here is another lifeless pile of words – sentence parts without a verb to make them into a live sentence:

Spacewoman Stella   on another mission at the same time next week.

- First, think of a main verb to add to it.
- Now change the main verb you've chosen for a completely different one.
- Now choose an auxiliary verb which you can use to make it clear that what is happening in this sentence *has* to happen.
- Now choose another auxiliary verb which you can use to make it clear that you're not exactly sure *if* this thing will happen.

14 How words change

A language shows that it is alive and healthy by constantly changing and growing. Over time, language changes in all kinds of ways – spelling, pronunciation, grammar and so on. The most obvious and the most rapid developments, however, are in the use and meaning of words and expressions. The words in a language can change in three ways:

■ New words appear to go with new ideas and inventions. For example:

a *pop promo* is a video made to promote a singer, band or record. Pop promo first appeared in English in the 1980s.

■ Old words disappear because they are no longer of use to anyone or they are replaced by more modern words. The words have become *obsolete*. For example:

we no longer use the word *wight* (a person) which was part of English four hundred years ago. Wight is now obsolete.

■ Words stay in the language, but their meaning changes. For example:

Chaucer describes one of the characters in 'The Canterbury Tales' as a *lusty bachelor*. We still use these words today, but with different meanings. In Chaucer's time, *lusty* meant happy and full of high spirits, while a *bachelor* was a young man who was training to become a knight.

In the time of William Shakespeare (1564–1616), people travelled on foot, by horse or by boat. There were no cars, bikes, motor-bikes, hovercraft, helicopters, and so there were no words for them. Although 70 per cent of our present-day English vocabulary was already in use by the time Shakespeare was writing his plays and sonnets, we would come up against all kinds of difficulties if we used only the words used by Shakespeare. We would have no words for all the ideas and objects that have been produced in the last 500 years!

> 1   Jot down twenty words we use today that people living at the time of Shakespeare would not have known. For example:
>   motorway

Some words and expressions enter and leave the *spoken* language within a short time. They come into fashion, the fashion changes and they disappear or their meaning changes. You can see this most clearly in the words people use to voice their approval of something or to express pleasure.

In the 1960s young people tended to use *swinging*, *fabulous*, *switched-on*, *with-it* or *smooth* when they thought something was really good. In the 1970s, *great* and *trendy* were popular words of approval. In the 1980s, words like *ace*, *magic*, *brill* and *wicked* had taken over as the words of the moment.

2   Draw up a list of the words and expressions you use when you really like something and approve of it, and the words you use when you really dislike or disapprove of something. For example:

	Like/approve	**Dislike/disapprove**
1990s	rad	gross

Most new words come into English in one of three ways:

■ They are adapted from old or established words. For example:

a computer that is easy to use is described as *user-friendly*. Friendly is a well-established word, but by adding it to the end of another word, a new word was created.

3   Show that you understand each of the following words by using them in sentences of your own:
environment-friendly
girl-friendly
customer-friendly

■ They are made up from words taken from other languages. For example:

telephone is made up from two ancient Greek words, *tele* meaning 'far off' and *phone* meaning 'sound'.

NB: You will find out more about words created in this way in Skills Session 3 on the roots of words on page 159.

■ They are borrowed directly from other languages. For example:

garage is borrowed from French.

4   Below is a list of words borrowed from other languages. Using an **etymological** dictionary, find out which language each word comes from.
ballot   bandit   glasnost   gong   kiosk

sofa   tea   tycoon   verandah   yacht

5   *Spaghetti, kebab, pizza, frankfurter, chow mein,* and *tandoori* are all new words that have come into English from other languages. On your own or in small groups, jot down as many words as you can that are connected with food that have been borrowed from other languages. If possible, write down the language that each word has come from. For example:
croissant (French)

15 Create the impression you want

It's you who chooses the words you use, in writing and in speaking. And you can choose the impression you want to make on people. For instance, if you're talking or writing about yourself, you can choose whether you want people to think that:

■ you're tough, and you don't care about things that happen to you; or
■ you're sad, and need sympathy.

This is a skill you probably learnt to use first of all when you were very young – getting people to feel sorry for you when you were in trouble, or showing how brave you were when you felt like crying. When you were young you did this by the things you *said*. Now that you're older, this is a skill you can begin to use in your *writing*.

Creating the impression you want is a skill that can be used in any kind of writing – even diaries, for instance. Diaries are supposed to be private, but even when we're writing in our diaries we sometimes take care to create the impression we want – just in case one day somebody happens to read what we've written.

Look at the following two examples of diary entries about the same event. How do these two versions create different impressions?

■ Tuesday. Sat next to Pete in Science. He looked fed up. We chatted about the end-of-term disco. I felt really sorry for him, because I'd heard he had nobody to go with. So I asked him if he'd like to go with me, but he said he was going with Sharon. Quite a relief really – for a moment it looked like I'd actually have to go with him myself! I think he fancies himself a bit.

■ Tuesday. Sat next to Pete in Science. All through the lesson I was dying to ask him if he'd go to the end-of-term disco with me. I've been wanting to ask him for ages. When we were clearing up at the end of the lesson, I summoned up the nerve to ask him finally. He looked really pleased with himself and said he was going with Sharon, of all people. I felt really stupid. If I can't go with him then it's not worth going at all. What's wrong with me?

Imagine that today, you've finally summoned up the nerve to ask someone you like a lot to come out with you. Unfortunately, the person says no. Write two different diary entries about what happened which create different impressions about how you felt, depending on how you choose to make people feel about you:
First version: write a diary entry that protects your pride – so that it looks like you don't mind about this at all.
Second version: without changing the facts of what happened, write a second diary entry that would make people feel sorry for you – so that it makes people feel that they want to look after you and comfort you.

It doesn't matter what you're writing. Whether it's a diary, a letter, a story, or a newspaper article – if you are doing the writing, then you can choose the words that create the impression you want.

16 How to interview people

There is a skill to interviewing people. It takes skill to:

- ask the right questions;
- listen to what people tell you;
- respond to what people tell you;
- make people feel relaxed, and open.

1   Start straightaway by interviewing each other about *favourite leisure activities* – that might be pop music, fishing, watching TV, football, computers, reading books, buying clothes, or anything else the person being interviewed likes doing and knows a lot about.

Work in groups of three – one of you interviewing, one being interviewed, and one watching and listening carefully, and taking notes about what goes on during the interview. Afterwards, discuss how the interview went.
- Was the person being interviewed relaxed, and able to talk freely?
- Did the person being interviewed tell the interviewer what she/he wanted to know?
- Was the interview like a pleasant conversation, or a nervous interrogation?

A successful interview depends mainly on the interviewer. It's up to the interviewer to make it easy for the person being interviewed to talk.

- Know the sorts of thing you want to find out before the interview begins – know *why* you're doing the interview.
- Think about questions before the interview begins – questions that will give the interviewee a chance to talk.
  Instead of asking *Do you like pop music?*, which makes it hard to say anything but *yes* or *no*, you could ask *What pop music do you like?* or *Tell me about your favourite pop records.*
  These are open questions, which allow people to talk freely, in more interesting ways.
- Be friendly, relaxed and encouraging throughout the interview. Smile, nod and look interested in what the person being interviewed says.
- Listen carefully to what is being said rather than thinking about your own next question all the time.
- As the interview goes on, and the person being interviewed begins to tell you things, ask follow-up questions, like:

  When you say that you like most pop groups except Bros, what do you mean?
  Why don't you like Bros?

2   Discuss how the first interview could have been improved by doing any of the above things. Carry out two more interviews: swop round roles – a different one of you doing the interviewing, a different one being interviewed, and a different one observing the interview each time.

17 Metaphors and similes

Metaphors

'I can't do any more work tonight. My batteries are completely flat.' This could mean that my personal stereo has ground to a halt, or it could mean that I'm really tired.
You've got to think twice about it because I'm using a **metaphor**. Metaphors are examples of what something means, or how something feels, that you have to think twice about, when you hear them or read them. Successful metaphors surprise you into thinking twice.

A lot of the time, we use metaphors that have been around a long time, and don't surprise us any more. They've become part of the language:

'I could eat a horse'   'he's a real pig'   'a blanket of snow'

There's nothing wrong with using language like this. People know what it means immediately. It's very convenient. But if you want to make people notice what you're saying, you need to find a really *surprising* way of saying what you mean.

Similes

'He's a real pig' is a metaphor: it's a way of speaking that involves pretending that what you're saying is literally true.

'He's *like* a pig' and 'he's *as* greedy as a pig' are **similes**. Similes involve admitting that what you're saying is not literally true – you're just saying that what you're describing is *like* something else.

It isn't always enough to find surprising examples of what you mean, or how something feels. Metaphors and similes need to be *suitable* as well. Look at this simile, for instance:

'My love is as big as a bus-station.'

That would certainly be a surprising thing to say, and bus-stations are certainly quite big – but maybe it's not really all that romantic. Perhaps it wouldn't be entirely suitable.

Invent brand new metaphors or similes, that are both surprising enough to make people think twice about what you're saying, and suitable enough to help them really understand what you mean, for each of these two situations:

- Imagine that you are away from home, feeling very lonely and homesick. Write a paragraph from a letter home, using a really surprising and suitable metaphor or simile to show just how utterly lonely you really feel.

- Imagine that you're trying to convince people that the factory-farming of chickens is very cruel. Think of a brand new metaphor or simile that is both surprising and suitable which will make them think hard about that kind of cruelty.

18 Adverbs

Spacewoman Stella *goes* to a new planet every week.

The **verb** tells us what's *happening* in this sentence – '*going* to a planet'. A verb gives you information about *what's happening* in a sentence. An **adverb** adds to that information, telling you *how* things are happening.

Spacewoman Stella goes *cheerfully* to a new planet every week.

The adverb in this sentence tells us *how* Stella goes. To find out if a word is an adverb, ask these questions:

> *What* is happening in this sentence? answer = **verb** (Stella *goes* to a new planet).
> *How* is it happening? answer = **adverb** (Stella goes *cheerfully* to a new planet).

USEFUL TIP: If the word you find, when you're looking for adverbs in this way, also ends in –*ly*, it is doubly likely to be an adverb.

Read the following passage, and carry out the language command that follows it:

It was a typical day aboard the Spaceship Encounter. Stella woke brightly from a long night's sleep, and leapt lightly out of bed. She looked straight into her mirror, and softly rubbed the sleep out of her eyes.

"You're hardly ageing at all, Stella old girl," she muttered to herself, humorously.

After breakfasting yummily on wheat cakes and camomile tea for the three thousandth time in her space-going career, Stella turned her attention eagerly to her TV screen.

"Ok," she said expectantly to her on-board computer, Melanie, "what movie have we got today, then?"

"Rambo Rules the Universe," suggested Melanie, helpfully.

"Oh that's just great," replied Stella rapturously. "That's just what I need."

And so one more day passed by, as swiftly as all the others.

Language command – find and write down all adverbs

1 Find the verbs in each sentence – the words that tell you what is *happening* in each sentence.

2 Look for, and write down, any words that tell you how that verb is happening – how what is going on in this sentence is happening, The words you choose are all likely to be adverbs.

3 See if the words you choose in answer to question 2 end in –*ly*. If they do, they are almost certainly adverbs (but not *all* adverbs end in –ly).

4 Replace all the adverbs in this passage with different ones, in order to change the mood of this passage from *cheerful* to *miserable*. For example, you could change 'Stella woke *brightly*' to *Stella woke grumpily*', and so on through the passage.

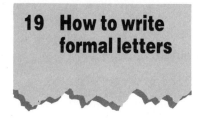

19 How to write formal letters

formal means → being serious, sensible, solemn
→ following agreed rules of behaviour

There are often times when we are expected to use language – speaking or writing – in a formal way at school, in work, on special occasions.

When speaking, that usually means:

- using Standard English (see ***Different kinds of English***) – avoiding slang and chatty language;
- speaking carefully, perhaps politely.

When writing, that usually means:

- following the rules of written Standard English;
- writing in a calm and reasoned way – not getting worked up;
- laying out your writing on the page following agreed rules of presentation.

As you grow up, and begin to take your place in the adult world, you will sometimes need to do one kind of formal writing in particular. You'll need to write formal letters:

- to apply for jobs;
- to arrange things with officials – writing to bank managers, local government officers, insurance companies, solicitors;
- to express your feeling and opinions about serious matters – to Members of Parliament, headteachers, government officials, business companies and organisations that provide important services.

If you want people to pay attention to you – if you want your opinions, requests or needs to be noticed – you ought to know how to write letters in a way that can't be ignored, in a formal way. Sometimes you might decide that a formal letter is not going to work. It's your choice – so long as you know *how* to write formal letters, and *when* you are expected to write them.

On the next page there are two short examples of formal letters. The letters you write can be much longer. These examples simply show you:

- the kind of language formal letters use;
- the way that they can be laid out.

It is quite simple to follow this kind of layout. It is just a matter of copying the way it is done. In addition, you need to think about these things:

- When do you need to write a formal letter?
- What kinds of words sound formal enough for the purposes of a particular letter?
- How formal do you want to be, for the purposes of a particular letter?

Write a letter to an imaginary bank manager asking politely but confidently – and formally – for a loan of £5,000. Think carefully about: layout, language, tone of voice.

Seaview,
12, Beach Road,
Tottingham,
Cumbria.

3 November, 1991

The Manager,
Cumbrian Water Company,
Cumbria.

Dear Sir or Madam,

I am writing to express my concern about the poor quality of drinking water currently provided, at some considerable cost, by your company.

The water we receive from our taps at present is muddy in colour, with an odd and rather unpleasant smell. Several members of my family have recently complained of nausea and giddiness after drinking this water, with the result that we now drink only expensive bottled water.

I would appreciate some reassurance from you on this matter at the earliest opportunity. Could you please explain what has gone wrong with our water, and what you are doing to improve the situation?

I am also quite naturally unhappy about having to pay for the high costs of water that I cannot use, and would appreciate some response from you on the question of refunds, and reduced bills in the future – at least until our water becomes acceptable again,

I look forward to a prompt reply.

Yours faithfully,

Ms. B. Taylor

Seaview,
12, Beach Road,
Tottingham,
Cumbria.

29 June, 1991

Mrs F. Guthrie
Personnel Officer,
Advanced Electronics Ltd.,
Upwardly Mobile Tower,
Manchester.

Dear Mrs Guthrie,

I am interested in the post of computer operator with your company, advertised in today's Guardian. Please will you send me an application form, and further details about the post? I enclose a stamped addressed envelope.

Yours sincerely,

Ms. B. Taylor

20 Choose the right words for the job

We all have to choose our words with care, from time to time. This is specially true out in the world of work, when we have to take care with people's feelings, or we have to make things very clear. We have to choose the right words for the job – thinking carefully about *what* we're trying to say, and *who* we're saying it to. Look at this example:

The new Headteacher at Coltrane Comprehensive School has only been in the job for a week, and already she's got a lot of problems to deal with:

- some teachers have been arriving late and failing to take the register;
- half the pupils in the school refuse to wear school uniform;
- the kitchen staff have gone on strike because of the rude things some teachers and pupils have been saying about the food;
- everyone keeps telling her how wonderful the last head was, and how much they miss him.

Write the letters that she would need to write, as part of her job, to keep things running smoothly. The examples show you the start of each piece she writes, and give you some idea of the kind of writing that is appropriate for the particular task.

1 · A memo to staff about the need to arrive on time, and about the importance of completing the register every day.

Memo to all staff

It has come to my notice, during the first week of this term, that certain colleagues have not been arriving in proper time for the start of the school day. I am sure that colleagues are aware that . . .

The special thing about this is that you must be both polite and strict at the same time.

2 A notice to be read out in registration, firmly instructing pupils on the fact that they must wear school uniform.

Notice to all pupils

I am extremely shocked and disappointed to discover that a large number of pupils are . . .

You can be a lot more direct, and less polite, when you are addressing pupils.

3   A letter to the person in charge of the kitchens, apologising for the nasty things people said about the food, and persuading her to get her staff back to work.

Dear Mrs White,
I really was most sorry to hear of the deeply unfair remarks that some

Sweet words might not butter any parsnips, but they're all you've got, so you'll have to use them very carefully here.

4   A letter to her mum, telling her how miserable she is in her new job.

Dear Mum,
I'm really having a horrible time, Mum. Nobody likes me and . . .

You can say exactly what you think to your mum, even when you're a headteacher.

It's not what you say that matters – it's the way you say it that makes the difference.

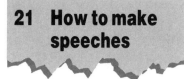

21 How to make speeches

You can learn some quite easy methods for making a speech that really gets an audience on your side: simple tricks of language that can make people really enthusiastic about what you're saying to them.

1   Imagine that you are in a school that has become very seriously short of money, and that the place is falling to bits. Write a short speech that could be delivered to fellow pupils – in assembly, or at a school council meeting – that gets them on your side in a campaign to improve something in the school, like:

■ the desks and chairs you have to use;
■ the lighting and decoration in classrooms and common rooms;
■ the school toilets.

People who make speeches for a living – like politicians – know how to make audiences want to start clapping at the right moments.

The following two applause tricks can succeed in getting people to clap you wildly *IF* you use them in the right way:

Trick one: use a two-part contrast

'What do YOU prefer to eat?
Clammy cod and mushy mash
OR sizzling chips and succulent sausages?

The trick here is to make whatever you're saying sound good by telling the audience about something bad first – by *contrasting* the two things.

Trick two: use a list of three things

'So, I say to you, if we start eating school meals again, we insist that we are given –
no more soggy chips
no more cold custard
and no more burnt burgers!!

Two things aren't enough, four are too many. People usually get most enthusiastic when they hear the *third* thing in a list of three – if it's delivered in a dramatic way.

Other speech-making skills

To make either of these two applause tricks work, you'll need to use certain other speech-making skills along with them:

- strong voice, varied voice;
- *us and them* language – talk to the audience as if you were all on the same side;
- think about the *sound* of your words: use tricks like **alliteration** – uSe Several wordS in the Same SentenCe with the Same Sound (SiZZling chipS and Succulent SauSageS);
- relaxed, confident body movements; forceful arm and hand gestures; firm, confident eye-contact with the audience.

2 Rewrite the short speech you wrote at the start of this Skills Session with at least two opportunities for applause written in – one in the middle, and one at the end. Each time, use one of the applause tricks described in this Skills Session. Practise delivering the finished speech to each other, using the other speech-making skills described above.

glossary

academic writing   serious, thoughtful kinds of writing, usually done in schools or universities, which people use for the purposes of explaining and understanding complicated things

accents   the different ways we *pronounce the sounds* of language – it is possible to use both Standard and non-standard English with any **accent**

alliteration   a sound effect used in poetry, advertising and journalism, which involves using the same sound at the beginning of several words in the same sentence, for example: *Really Revolting Rubbish*

anecdote   a very short story about something that happened to you, or that you heard about – usually told to illustrate something being discussed in a conversation

appropriate language   language that is *right* for a particular *purpose*, that is *acceptable*, is **appropriate** (see **formal** and **informal language**)

autobiography   telling the story of your own life, or of selected parts of your own life, in whatever way you choose

blurb   the short piece of writing on the cover of a book that tells people how good that particular book is

conventions   rules of behaviour that most people follow for the sake of convenience, *because* they're what most people follow. Language has many conventions – such as **spelling** and **speech punctuation**

dialect   the name for a particular version of the English language, with its own vocabulary or special uses of grammar, that is spoken by a particular group of people, or in a particular part of the country. *Not* to be confused with **accent**, which is simply the way people **pronounce** words

dialogue   in stories, or plays, this is when characters talk to each other

draft   an attempt to put words onto paper. When we write, we often need to draft things more than once, as we work out exactly what we want to say

etymology   the history of words – where words come from, and how they change over time

fictional   made-up, imaginary, invented

formal language   language that is both *serious* and *sensible*, and that follows certain agreed rules, or conventions. Language that is used in certain situations, like taking exams, job interviews, and talking to important people – wherever it is **appropriate**

formula   a fixed way of doing things or understanding things that one can stick to and rely on

grammar   grammar is the name for the *mechanics*, the *systems*, of language. The ways in which words are put together into sentences in order to make sense

informal language   language that is easy-going and casual, and which doesn't follow strict rules. Langage that is used between friends, and whenever we don't need to worry about making the right impression

impersonal writing   writing that appears to tell you about facts, and *not* about the feelings or opinions of the person writing it

ingredients   stories are like meals – different types of stories (horror stories, love stories, adventure stories) each have their own special **ingredients**. For example, the typical **ingredients** of a *horror story* are often *spooky castles, graveyards, creaking doors* and *thunder storms*

local words   words that are only used in one particular part of the country, or even only in one particular town or village. Some local words are hundreds of years old, and some have recently been invented. For example, there are many different words for *newt* in different parts of England, such as *effet, padgetty-poll, swift, tiddly-winks,* and *yolt*

layout   the way writing is arranged on the page, in order to be attractive, clear and easy to follow. Layout involves thoughtful use of *headings, spaces, paragraphs* and *emphasis*

literally   if we say that something is **literally** true, we mean that it is genuinely true in real life

Middle English   The version of the English language that was used during the middle ages. It was a mixture of Old English and French, and was used most during the fourteenth and fifteenth centuries. Modern English grew out of it during the following centuries

metaphor   a surprising but suitable example of what something means or feels like. **Metaphors** are used as if they were *literally* true, for example: *my sister's a butterfly* (see **simile**)

non-standard English   ways of speaking or writing that are different from the official version used in education, official activities and most writing

narrative   the way the events of a story are put into a particular order and told to a reader or an audience

narrator   every story – every **narrative** – is *told* by someone, who might be real or fictional. The **narrator** is the person who tells you a story, who talks to you from the page

Old English   the language spoken in England during the period from the fifth to the twelfth centuries. It was made up mainly from languages used by invaders from Scandinavia – the Angles, Saxons and Jutes. It is sometimes called Anglo-Saxon

obsolete   words that were once used a lot but that people have now finished with, and forgotten. Words which can only be found in dictionaries

paragraphs   one of the most important ways of *organising* writing – you start up new paragraphs for each new step or stage in stories and essays

playscript   the special way of laying out a narrative or story so that people can act it out – it shows clearly who is speaking and what they say – any information about what they are actually doing is provided as stage directions, in brackets

prose all writing, apart from *verse* and *notes*

punctuation the marks used for controlling words on the page, and for making them easier to follow and understand – like *full stops, commas, colons* and *question marks*

regional accents the accents of different areas of the United Kingdom, for example: *Scouse* (Liverpool), *cockney* (London), *Geordie* (north-east England), *Yorkshire, Lancashire, Somerset*

register the name for a particular way of using language, and choosing **vocabulary**, that occurs in special situations – like in education, law, sport, pop music, religion

role play acting a role in an imaginary situation, as if it was real, in order to learn something about what that situation is like

setting the place and time in which a particular story takes place. The **setting** of *Neighbours*, for instance, is a suburban street in Australia during the present

simile a striking and suitable example of what something means or feels like. **Similes** make it clear that what you're saying isn't literally true, for example: *my sister's like a butterfly* (see **metaphor**)

slang the unofficial, informal language of different groups – it is used as a private way of talking between members of that group (for instance, young people at school), and in order to keep others out. Slang is often disapproved of by outsiders

Standard English the version of England that you are taught in school, and which is used for writing and official purposes. It is also sometimes called **correct English**, and the **Queen's English**

standardised when one particular dialect of the language becomes the official version of the language, it gets **standardised**. People agree on how it should be used – how it should be spelt, what the rules of grammar are, and what words are acceptable in it. It can take hundreds of years for a language to become standardised

transcript a *written-down* version of exactly what people said during a conversation, discussion or interview. **Transcripts** are usually made from tape-recordings, or short-hand notes

tabloid small, handy-sized newspapers like the *Sun*, the *Mirror*, the *Daily Mail*, the *Sunday Sport*

vocabulary the *full* range of words available to all of us in the language. Nobody knows the whole **vocabulary** of their own language, which is why we have *dictionaries*, where we can find out the meaning of *specialist*, *technical* or unusual words